ETERNITY REALIZED

Robert Philip (1791-1858)

ETERNITY REALIZED
A GUIDE TO THE THOUGHTFUL

BY ROBERT PHILIP

REFORMATION HERITAGE BOOKS
Grand Rapids, Michigan

Biographical Foreword
Copyright © 2007
Joel R. Beeke and Jay T. Collier

Published by
Reformation Heritage Books
2965 Leonard St., NE
Grand Rapids, MI 49525
616-977-0599 / Fax 616-285-3246
e-mail: orders@heritagebooks.org
website: www.heritagebooks.org

ISBN #978-1-60178-007-2

Reprinted from first American edition
Boston: Perkins & Marvin, 1833

*For additional Reformed literature, both new and used,
request a free book list from the above address.*

Biographical Foreword

The books of Robert Philip were very popular in nineteenth-century Great Britain and America for their practical guidance on promoting personal, Reformed piety. A biblical, heartwarming spirituality glowed from their pages; the reader's attention was drawn to God's storehouse of divine comforts. Today, Philip has become relatively unknown, and his works have faded into obscurity. Having recently republished *Communion with God* and *The Love of the Spirit Traced in His Works*, this book is our third effort to bring Philip's excellent writings back to light.

Robert Philip was born in Huntly, Aberdeenshire, Scotland, in May of 1791. His father was an elder in a Congregational church pastored by George Cowie, well-known as "the Whitefield of northern Scotland." Young Robert grew up in a vibrant, evangelistic church of Puritan persuasion and in the company of some of the most important leaders of Independency in Scotland. After his father's death in 1806, he moved to Aberdeen, where he acquired a job as a clerk and became a member of the Belmont Congregational Church. His pastor there, Dr. John Philip (no relation), encouraged him to pursue gospel ministry, and provided him preparatory studies before entering more formal training.

In 1811, Robert Philip began his theological studies at Hoxton Academy in London, under the guidance of its president, Dr. Robert Simpson, known as "a man of God mighty in prayer." Philip assumed his first pastorate in 1815 for the Newbington Chapel in Liverpool. His labors there were characterized by an intense desire to be "made all things to all men," so that he "might by all means save some" (1 Cor. 9:22). Being a port town, Liverpool was an ideal place for ministry to sailors.

Philip recognized the neglect shown to this class of men, and made it his mission to reach them with the gospel. He familiarized himself with seafaring events in order to gain their respect, and published a series of his addresses to sailors as *The Bethel Flag; or, Sermons to Seamen*.

Meanwhile, in 1818, Philip married Hannah Lassel of Bolton, Lancashire. In 1826, the Philips moved to London, where Robert Philip spent the next thirty years as minister of Maberly Chapel. Here he often preached up to four times on a Sunday, twice in his own congregation and once or twice elsewhere. He developed a greater focus on experiential Christianity and piety, which he found to be more effective in building up a healthy church than his earlier efforts.

Philip authored a series of *Experimental Guides* and two series of books intended for young men and women, eventually collected under the titles *The Young Man's Closet Library* and *The Young Lady's Closet Library*, all of which promoted a healthy spirituality among evangelical Christians through simple, earnest, and practical writing. He also produced works on Richard Baxter, George Whitefield, John Bunyan, William Milne, and John Campbell, which gave Christian biography a devotional turn. One of Philip's final and most helpful books, *The Eternal; or, the God of Our Fathers*, was the outgrowth of a series of Sunday morning sermons on the attributes of God. In all of these books, Philip demonstrates a great indebtedness to the Puritans and a drive to see their experiential Christianity flourish in the context of his own day.

Tributes to Philip's writing came from many quarters, including the *British Quarterly Review*, *Literary World*, *Christian Age*, *Eclectic Review*, *Evangelical Magazine*, *Sword and Trowel*, and *Glasgow Herald*. The *Edinburgh Daily Review* wrote, "His style is clear and earnest, and his thoughts always practical in their bearing.... They display great beauty and tenderness of composition." The *American Literary Advocate* claimed that "no modern theological works are so widely circulated amongst all denominations in America as Mr. Philip's."

Philip also dedicated himself to the promotion of foreign missions. He was especially drawn to China, and took several trips there on behalf of the London Missionary Society, of which he was eventually made director.

The early 1850s marked a decline in Philip's activity. After receiving an honorary doctorate of divinity from Dartmouth College in 1852, which was a significant recognition of his influence in the United States, Philip's work became confined to his pastoral duties. His health grew increasingly worse, leading him to resign from the pastorate at Maberly Chapel in 1855. He died at his home on May 1, 1858, and was buried in Abney Park cemetery.

Although written generations ago, we hope that Philip's books will be used by God for a renewal of experiential Christianity in our day. In *Eternity Realized: A Guide to the Thoughtful,* Philip guides the reader to the borders of Immanuel's land. Too often, Christians neglect the practice of being heavenly minded. Philip reminds us of our duty to meditate on heaven and the danger we place our soul in when we disregard this task. Yet, more than just pointing out a mere duty, Philip places key aspects of the Christian life in the light of eternity and gives practical helps in cultivating a delight in heavenly things. Read, ponder, and experience how developing the habit of realizing the eternal world to come will help you keep this world in its proper place.

— Joel R. Beeke and Jay T. Collier

CONTENTS

Chap.		Page
I.	Duty of Realizing Eternity	9
II.	The Possibility of Realizing Eternity	29
III.	The Excuses for not Realizing Eternity	45
IV.	Nominal Faith, from not Realizing Eternity	66
V.	Spititual Declension, from not Realizing Eternity	84
VI.	Faith, Believing unto Eternal Life	101
VII.	Eternity Realized in the Sanctuary	121
VIII.	Eternity Realized at the Sacrament	139
IX.	Eternity Realized at Home	157
X.	Christ, the Glory of Eternity	180

No. I.

THE DUTY OF REALIZING ETERNITY.

Did "Eternal Life" suggest to us only the bare idea of living for ever in an unknown world, it would deserve more attention than is usually given to heaven or hell. "The life that now is," is such an evanescent vapor, that "everlasting life," however deeply veiled as to its place or employments, is a contrast which ought to arrest and rivet supreme attention. The bare fact of immortality is fraught with instruction and warning. It has a commanding character, independent of its revealed character. For, as life involves thought, and feeling, and action; an eternity of thinking, an eternity of feeling, an eternity of acting, is a solemn consideration! It could not be weighed without profit. Who would not be improved, both in character and spirit, by arguing thus :—" I must *think* for ever; would an eternal train of my usual thoughts be either worthy of me, or useful to me? I must *feel* for ever; would an eternal reign of my present spirit and desires please me? I must *act* for ever; would an eternal course of my habitual conduct bring happiness, or even bear reflection?"

We could not bring our tastes and tempers to this test, without improving both. The moment we realize an eternity of any vice or folly, we are shocked. To be eternally passionate, or eternally sensual, or eternally covetous, or eternally capricious, is a state of being which must be appalling and repulsive even to the victims of these vices. Thus, independent of all the light shed upon immortality by the gospel, immortality itself sheds strong and steady lights upon our personal interests and relative duties. Life involves, also, society, intercourse, and their natural results. Would, then, an eternity of the terms and temper of our present domestic and social life be altogether agreeable to us? Should we like to "live for ever," just as we now "live together" at home? Would an eternity of our present feelings towards certain persons be either creditable or useful to us? Should we be quite satisfied to obtain and deserve, for ever, no more respect than we now enjoy? Would an immortality of our present relative condition please us? Here, again, by realizing an eternity of social life, we catch glimpses both of duty and interest, which compel "great searchings of heart," and suggest many valuable improvements of character.

It would, then, be equally unwise and criminal, not to realize even a veiled eternity. It would be both moral and mental weakness not to judge of our present character and pursuits—of our present spirit and habits—by their fitness and likelihood to please and profit us in a "world without end." What attention, then, is due to an unveiled and illuminated immortality; and, what an influence it might have over us, if habitually realized as it is revealed? It comes before us, in the gospel, as everlasting happiness in heaven, or as everlasting misery in hell; as an eternity in the presence of God, and in the fellowship of all the godlike spirits in the universe; or, as an eternity in the presence of "the devil and his angels," and in the society of all the impious and impure. Extremes, thus infinite and endless, deserve all the attention which law or gospel demands for them. Habitual remembrance of them would be imperative duty, if neither law nor gospel enforced it. Such an eternity makes many laws for itself. It is *itself* a law, and felt to be so when it is realized. For as Sinai awed the thousands of Israel, by its solemn aspect, long before the trumpet sounded, so the very aspect of eternal bliss or wo appeals to the understanding and the conscience, by its own solemnity.

Now we blame, as well as pity, those who banish the consideration of this unveiled immortality. We are thankful that we are not so mentally weak, as to be incapable of reflecting on the things which are "unseen and eternal;" nor so morally infatuated as to be utterly unaffected by them. We had rather lose one of our bodily senses, than be wholly insensible to the glories and solemnities of the world to come. We see clearly, and often feel deeply, that without some just sense of them, there cannot be a due appreciation of the claims of the law or the gospel, nor of the duties of life and godliness. These have all such an express reference to eternity, that if we were to think and act without any pointed reference to it, we durst not give ourselves credit either for believing or for understanding truth and duty.

This is well, so far. It is, however, one

thing to be unable or unwilling to forget eternity; and another, to *cultivate* the remembrance of it. We may not evade the prospect, when it is forced upon us by death in the family, or by appeals in the sanctuary; but, do we invite it, for its own sake, when there is neither accident nor excitement to constrain our attention? Is the contemplation of " the powers of the world to come," any part of our devotional and meditative habits? We voluntarily and conscientiously *give* some set time to prayer, and to self-examination, and to the study of the great principles of truth and duty. We do not allow our sense of them to depend entirely upon accident or excitement. We require, in order to keep up a good hope through grace, to examine and review the grounds of hope; and, in order to maintain a good conscience towards God and man, we require to confront conscience, from time to time, with the claims of both. But, do we require, for our own satisfaction and improvement, to set apart some time for the deliberate and distinct consideration of the claims of eternal life? They are, indeed, *mixed up* in our minds with the other claims of religion and morality, and give some degree of force to both; but, if they are rather admitted than meditated, rather taken for granted than weighed, we do not give that "good heed" to them which they demand and deserve.

The prospects of eternal life are revealed to us, that we may employ them to counterbalance the pressure of the sufferings and sorrows of "the life which now is." They were habitually employed for this purpose, by those who first believed that gospel which illuminated life and immortality. They did more than calculate, that all their trials were working together "for good." They reckoned, also, that their "affliction" was working for them "a far more exceeding and eternal weight of glory." They realized heaven so as to be relieved and refreshed by the anticipations of it. But what, in general, is our resource under suffering and sorrow? Alas! not this direct and distinct reckoning, that they are not "worthy to be compared with the glory which shall be revealed in us;" but reckoning, that good will come out of them, and that we shall see better days "in the land of the living." Better days in the land of the *dead*, are not much desired by us whilst we have any rational hope of life. I mean—that it is not by them, chiefly, we balance our troubles, whilst death does not seem inevitable nor at hand. There is, in fact, something dearer to us, at present, than heaven. We have no wish to be *soon* there, however much we desire or hope to be found there at last. Accordingly, the hope of glory is not often our chief consolation in the day of calamity.

Now this proves more, than that our personal hope is often low and fluctuating. It proves, also, that we are not very familiar with the objects of future happiness. Indeed, one great cause of that lowness and changeableness of our hope of heaven is, our inattention to heaven itself. It is not often nor minutely contemplated, exactly as it is set before us in the gospel. We do not overlook eternal things, but we do not "*look at*" them one by one, nor as a whole, sufficiently. We have no low nor foolish notions of heaven, but we have many vague, and not a few uninfluential, ideas of it. The reason is obvious: we have not taken the same time or care to acquaint ourselves with it, that we have taken to form and mature our acquaintance with the *way* which leads to it. Our knowledge of "the way that leadeth to everlasting life" is not, indeed, perfect; but still, it is influential. We prize our deliberate views and convictions of the glory and grace of the atonement; we can make something of them, and sometimes *much*, in the day of trouble; and they *tell* well upon our character and spirit even in the day of prosperity. So does our general idea of heaven; but not so the *details* of our knowledge of it; they have not much influence. How could they? The greater part of them have no fixed nor definite character or form in our minds. Were our views of the doctrines of grace as vague as many of our opinions about glory are, we should feel ashamed of ourselves, and be far more uncomfortable than we are now.

Whatever scrutiny or remonstrance breathes in these remarks, is not uncalled for by the usual state of our minds. Slight views of eternal life, are one great cause of our slight hold on the hope of salvation. A deeper acquaintance with immortality, in all its revealed forms, would compel us to take and keep a firmer grasp of the cross. Were we daily " looking for the mercy of our Lord Jesus Christ *unto eternal life,*" as well as unto a holy and tranquil life, both our faith and prayers would breathe another spirit than they usually do; and thus we should soon have no occasion for the common complaint, that our hope of heaven is too weak to weigh much against the trials of life. Let eternity dictate the *measure of faith* in Christ which its own solemnity deserves; and this will lead to such solid building, and to such steady resting upon the Rock of Ages, that we shall soon have a hope so full of immortality, that, like the first believers, we shall be able to counterbalance the things which are seen and temporal, by the things which are unseen and eternal. And, surely, if the martyrs could do so, we well may, under our lighter afflictions. It is, therefore, our own interest to acquire such a hold upon heaven, as shall really be of *use* to us in the time of trouble. Nothing aggravates trouble so much as a dark cloud on our eternal prospects. We have need of all our time and strength for the due exercise of patience and resignation in the evil day, instead of having to clear up, then, the agitating question of personal safety. Let us not, therefore, believe the gospel so vaguely and vapidly now, nor obey the law so partially now, that when the dark side of the pillar of time turns upon us, the dark side of the pillar of eternity should turn upon us too. There is no occasion for such a conjunction, as the fear of "the blackness of darkness," blending with the clouds of temporal calamity.

We owe it also unto others to cultivate such a hope of glory, as shall have a visible influence upon our *spirits*, as well as upon our character; and upon our *conversation*, as well as our conduct. Without worth of character, no testimony to the worth of religion will have any weight in our family, or social circle. It is not enough, however, that both our careless and undecided friends should be constrained, by our general character, to conclude, " that if any get to heaven we shall." Our *words*, as well as our works, should aid in lodging this conviction in their minds. We ought to *speak* of our " inheritance with the saints in light," as well as cultivate meetness for it. The first believers not only thought of heaven, and prepared for it, they also avowed and proclaimed the pleasure they found in looking forward to it as rest from their labors, and as freedom from their imperfections. They did not leave the inference of their safety to be drawn by others only; they drew it themselves also. They were wise enough, and manly enough, to judge, that a character and spirit which even the enemies of the gospel could not quote against the gospel, warranted them to consider themselves as heirs of eternal life. They did not, therefore, allow it to depend on the candor and conscience of others, whether this conclusion should be drawn or not. It was too important to be left to public caprice; and, therefore, they drew it themselves. "We, according to his promise, look for new heavens and a new earth." "We know that if our earthly house of this tabernacle were dissolved, we have a building of God, an house not made with hands, eternal in the heavens." "As we have borne the image of the earthly, we shall also bear the image of the heavenly." This was speaking *out*, on the subject of Christian hope! Yes; and yet it was saying no more than God had warranted. It is only what all may and ought to avow, who are relying on Christ for a holy salvation.

Now such a testimony, when not contradicted by the character of the witness, could not fail to commend the gospel. It would bring our relations and friends to the point. "Here," they must confess, "is *present* happiness, as well as a strong probability of eternal happiness." Whereas, if they see us in almost as much doubt of our future safety, as they are of their own, they will question the use of *faith*, even if they do not question the use of good works.

Silence is, however, so common on this

subject, and so characteristic of those who are most warranted to speak out, that it seems almost a virtue. We are so accustomed to entire silence, or to vague expressions, about personal expectations of heaven, that we should be almost *startled* to hear even the best of our pious friends, who are neither old nor infirm, avow their pleasure or hope. There must be very eminent piety indeed, in the person to whom we could listen, with common patience, whilst he was speaking of his own crown or mansion of glory. Free and firm statements of this kind, we should be ready to set down as ominous symptoms of a speedy death, whatever were the health, or the age, or the holiness of the person who made them. And, in our own case, and that of Christians in general, we should consider it a want both of humility and prudence, to utter our hopes of heaven, even when they are strongest. We act thus towards our nearest friends: and in the case of the world, we are induced to say, that it would be casting " pearls before swine," to tell worldly men that we had found a title to heaven in the atonement of Christ. We almost give our " consent," that he who says so to others, before he is upon his death-bed, should be laughed at by the world, and suspected by the church.

This is the current feeling on the subject now. It was not so in the olden time. Then, Christians comforted one another under their trials, with the comfortable words, " we shall meet the Lord in the air, and so shall we ever be with the Lord." And are we *wiser* or *humbler* than the first believers? Were they presumptuous or imprudent when they said, in the presence of the world, " Blessed be the God and Father of our Lord Jesus Christ, who, according to his abundant mercy, hath begotten us again unto a lively hope, by the resurrection of Jesus Christ from the dead, to an inheritance incorruptible, and undefiled, and that fadeth not away." Is this language, or our silence, most in harmony with the spirit of the gospel? Was their triumph, or is our timidity, the best way of commending the gospel? One thing is certain,—their rejoicing in Christ Jesus, and in the hope of eternal life, had a mighty influence, both in explaining and endearing the gospel to their friends and neighbors. Even their persecutors often dropped the sword, the axe, and the torch of martyrdom, overcome by the holy triumphs of the martyrs, and suffered with the victims they came to destroy.

But these were extraordinary times! True. The gospel is, however, the same in our "day" that it was in their "yesterday." And, whatever higher degree of glory we are willing to concede to the martyrs and confessors, we expect the same heaven. And shall we be ashamed to say so? Can our silence do good to ourselves, or to any one else? It will certainly never be an effectual check to Antinomian boasting. If that "unclean spirit" is ever cast out of the churches, it must be by the prevalence of a hope as full of immortality as of good fruits. For, until believers acquire and acknowledge as much comfort from the *revealed* will of God, as Antinomianism pretends to furnish from the *secret* purposes of God, the boasting will go on. The silence of believers, has, in fact, done much to create and keep up the loquacity of that system. Its high pretensions are just the opposite extreme of our silent and low hopes. Antinomians say too much, and we say too little; and thus we furnish them, however unintentionally, with plausible arguments against our principles.

This is not a light matter. We are held up

as being legalists, and unbelievers, and traitors to the doctrines of grace. Now, any one can despise this charge; or, by argument, refute it. It has often been triumphantly refuted and retorted. But, still it is kept up. And, O say not, "*What does it signify?*" nor, "*Who cares what Antinomians think or say?*" It does signify, and we ought to care; for the change is founded, chiefly, upon our acknowledgments of doubt, and suspense, and want of comfort in religion; and it is not answered when we say, that our low hopes prove nothing against our principles. This is, indeed, true; but it is equally true, that our low hopes, and frequent lack of comfort, prove that we, in some way or degree, *misapprehend* the gospel. For, as Christ expressly and repeatedly declares, that whosoever believeth on him "*hath everlasting life, and shall never perish;*" and, as we profess to believe on him, it is not altogether unfair nor unnatural, if those who see little and hear less of our hope of salvation, should both think and say that *unbelief* lies at the bottom of our silence and suspense. Indeed, they are right when they say so. They are far wrong when they call us *unbelievers;* but not very far from the truth when they charge us with unbelief. We certainly do not believe that we "have eternal life," when we indulge or express the fear of perishing. That hope, and this fear, are incompatible. The fear is not, indeed, incompatible with *faith*, but it is so with hope. John recognized, as true believers, those who did not know, for a time, that they had eternal life; and wrote to them that they "*might know*" that they had it. (1 John v. 13.) But he also told them, that "He that feareth is not made perfect in love; for perfect love casteth out (tormenting) fear."

For our own sake, therefore, and for the sake of others, and "for the truth's sake," we are solemnly bound to cherish such a hope of eternal life, as shall endear the gospel to ourselves, and commend it to others. But this we never can do, if eternal life itself is not made the subject of deliberate and devotional contemplation. Hasty, and partial, and occasional glances at heaven, will not call forth strong faith, nor bring into our minds such "forms of glory" as can delight the soul in the day of adversity, or sanctify it in the day of prosperity. Eternal things are *unseen* things, and therefore not to be apprehended or appreciated at once. Like the invisible God, they require us to "acquaint"

ourselves with them. Now, as it is not the
vague notion of God which is afloat in the world
that awes or animates our minds; but his revealed character as God in Christ, and that,
viewed in all its attributes, and often thought
of; so it is not the vague and meagre notion of
heaven as a mere place of safety from hell,
that can either set our affections on things
above, or soothe us amidst the vicissitudes of
things on the earth. We must meditate on
the character of eternity, as we have on the
character of God—deeply, frequently, voluntarily, if we would be influenced by it. In
like manner, whatever love we have to an unseen Saviour was not derived, and is not sustained, from the superficial ideas of him which
are afloat in the world; but from views of his
person and work, drawn from the divine testimony, compared with the opinions of the
apostles and prophets, harmonized with the
songs of angels and glorified spirits, and often
tried upon the fears of our heart and the
wounds of our spirit. Thus, whatever just
and influential estimate we have formed of the
divine favor, it has been drawn from scriptural views of the divine character. We *set
ourselves* to think over the character of God

and the Lamb, until it awake some hope, and even some love, in our minds. And now, we can set our knowledge of God and the Lamb against many of our fears and trials, with some success. Our convictions of the divine *wisdom* enable us to wait with some patience for "the end of the Lord" in our trials. And our convictions of the divine *faithfulness*, keep the promises precious in our estimation, even whilst they are not much fulfilled in our experience.

Here, then, there is some happy accordance between the influence which the invisible God and Saviour have over us, and that influence which they had over the first believers. We are, in some measure, of "one spirit" with them, in bringing the perfections of God and the blood of the Lamb to bear upon our hopes and fears. Why, then, are we so unlike them, in reckoning that the sufferings of the present time, are not worthy to be compared with the glory which shall be revealed in us? It is needless to ask, why do we not "desire to depart and be with Christ;" nor, why do we not "groan, earnestly desiring to be clothed upon with our house which is from heaven?" These questions would be evaded. But let us not evade the inquiry, Why have eternal things such a small place in our thoughts and conversation, compared to the "large room" they had in the hearts of the primitive Christians? We not only can make but little practical use of the prospects of heaven; but we are ashamed to speak, and often afraid to think of them. We might really dislike heaven, so little do we say about it; or be indifferent to it, so seldom do we set ourselves to contemplate it.

It is not, therefore, at all wonderful, however lamentable it may be, that we turn more to the doctrine of a *present* Providence for relief in the day of trouble, than to the doctrine of *future* glory. We have studied the former more than the latter. Had Providence engaged our attention as seldom and slightly as eternity has done, it would have had even less place in our minds, and less influence on our character, than eternity has. What, then, would be the happy effect of giving, for a time, such "good heed" to the whole doctrine of immortality, as we have done to the doctrines of grace and Providence? The revelation of glory will not divert us from the revelation of grace. The time required in order to our being well informed concerning the crown, will not render us ill affected towards the cross. A fair and full view of heaven will not cut any of the natural links of life, nor alienate the heart from any of the duties of life or godliness. These may be eclipsed for a moment by the superior claims of eternity; but, as in the eclipses of the sun and moon, the shadows will soon pass off, and leave all proper things in their proper place and power. There is no danger of so realizing the things which are unseen and eternal, as to forget the things which are seen and temporal. The danger is, lest the latter displace the former.

No. II.

THE POSSIBILITY OF REALIZING ETERNITY.

Whilst there is nothing we more readily admit than the grandeur and solemnity of eternity, there is, perhaps, nothing we are more reluctant to dwell on. We have, indeed, no objection to hear, occasionally, a well-timed and solemn-toned appeal to the awful realities of eternity; nor do we dislike those occasional gleams of it which flash upon our spirit when we are communing with God in prayer. We are rather pleased, than otherwise, to feel now and then that we are not insensible to the glories of heaven and the terrors of hell, nor altogether uninfluenced by them. Indeed we should question both the soundness and the sincerity of our faith, if it never realized "the things which are unseen and eternal," except when it was forced to do so by ministerial and providential appeals. Thus the subject has upon its side our understanding entirely, and our conscience too in no small degree.

This is, so far, well. It does not, however, disprove the assertion, that we are reluctant to cultivate realizing views of eternity. Deliberate efforts to acquire and keep up a solemn sense of eternal things are very rare; and not at all equal, in kind or degree, to the efforts we make in order to maintain a becoming sense of the evil of sin and the necessity of holiness. We are even afraid of an abiding impression of eternity; and suspect, if not believe, that it would throw a gloom over life, and turn seriousness into sadness. This lurking suspicion is not dislodged, nor much shaken, even when we remember that it is on the *bright* side of the pillar of eternity we are invited to dwell. We cannot forget that it has a *dark* side too, which may turn upon us oftener than we should like. And we see, with some clearness, that even on its bright side, we should be kept more familiar with death than we wish to be at present. We can hardly conceive it possible to think much of eternity, without thinking too much about death; they are so closely associated in our minds. The latter appears to us the dark shadow of the former, even when the former is brightest,

Thus there is against the habit of looking daily to eternal things all the natural and acquired force of our love of life, and of our fear of death. The claims of immortality present themselves to us, pointing to the grave, and muttering our mortality. We believe that Jesus Christ brought immortality to light; but, somehow, we *feel* that it is the king of terrors who holds up the prospect to us. Our "last enemy," rather than our best friend, is most seen, in connection with our glimpses of the invisible world.

There are also causes of reluctance, which are more discreditable to us. We see, at a glance, that an habitual sense of eternity would impose and compel more self-denial, or self-control, or self-examination, than we altogether like. We feel, instinctively, that certain tempers and tendencies, if not some habits also, would require great and immediate improvements, if they were confronted from day to day with the claims of Heaven. Every aspect of immortality is so full of solemn protests against all compromises with the flesh and the world, that even the most exemplary cannot but see clearly, and feel deeply, that they are not altogether that "manner of persons" which, as heirs of immortality, they ought to be.

These are not imaginary nor slight causes of that shrinking from the realization of eternity which is so common. We are eagle-eyed in discerning how a habit of realizing it would bring all our habits, public, domestic, and secret, under solemn revision and stricter discipline; and, thus, whatever is bad in our nature and character, as well as all that is weak in them, is averse to the duty, because it involves so many other duties.

It is this, much more than the difficulty of forming clear views of invisible realities, that prevents us from looking often to the things which are unseen and eternal. There are indeed, mental hindrances, but they are neither so many nor so great as the *moral* hindrances. This is self-evident from the single fact, that we understand enough of the nature both of heaven and hell to make and keep us intent upon reaching the former and escaping the latter. Our knowledge of them is not so dim nor indefinite, as to prevent us from prizing the great salvation. Were we, therefore, as intent upon present deliverance from all wrong habits and tempers, as upon future escape from the wrath to come, we should find our knowledge quite as sufficient to induce greater holiness, as it is to endear the cross. It looks ill, therefore, when we, who never complain, nor pretend, that our views of eternity are either too few or feeble to endear the atonement, pretend that we know too little of it to live under its direct influence. This does not tell well. That which binds us to the cross, notwithstanding all its mysteries and all its odium, could not fail, if equally applied to universal holiness, to bind us to it also. Besides (and let the fact prevent for ever, in our case, all attempts to shelter aversion under the wing of ignorance) we hope to die in triumph or tranquillity, upon the faith of what we know of heaven, both as a state and as a place. We are sure, and must confess, that if we can only *enjoy* then, all that we can anticipate and understand now, we shall not be strangers to comfort or composure when we come to exchange worlds. Away, then, with the pitiful pretence that our ideas of future glory are too indefinite to have an habitual influence upon our present character and spirit: they are, by our own acknowledgment, distinct enough, and numerous enough, to "turn the shadow of death into the morning," even when heart and flesh are failing. Surely, therefore, they are adequate, if honestly applied, to make all sin appear "exceeding sinful," and all holiness "altogether lovely."

Nothing is more unfounded (as will hereafter be shown) than the pretence that we know what heaven *is not*, rather than what *it is*. This is a poor compliment to Him, who "brought life and immortality to light, (illuminated them,) by the gospel." It is an equally mean and meagre commentary on this sublime fact, to say, that the future state is chiefly revealed to us by negatives. Both heaven and hell are revealed in the same way, and almost to the same extent, as the perfections of God, or the person and work of the Saviour. Negatives are as much used in explaining their character, as in depicting the invisible world, and are, in general, as useful, on both subjects, as the most positive information. We might, therefore, just as well say, that we do not know enough of God or the Lamb to think much about them, as say that we know too little of eternal things to think much about them. We do not, indeed, know all the truth concerning either, nor comprehend all that is revealed; but both are alike adapted to our capacity, and equally distinct. Accordingly, the claims of heaven upon our attention and affections, are as fully stated as the claims of the law or the gospel; and, what is more, the claims of God and the Lamb are chiefly enforced by the glories and terrors of eternity: facts which demonstrate that there is no lack of light, whatever lack of *looking* there may be.

It is not much wiser to refer to the *weakness* of our minds, when the duty of looking to the things which are unseen and eternal, is enforced upon us. It is, indeed, very plausible, and seems very humble, to ask, " What can we make of such a subject as eternity? We are lost the moment we attempt to realize it! Even in its barest form—that of endless duration—it defies all our calculations. We are no nearer to the comprehension of it, when we think of countless myriads of millions of ages, than when we think of countless moments. Like infinity, it has its centre everywhere; but its circumference nowhere. What then is the use of trying to comprehend the incomprehensible?"

All this, however, is equally true of God and the Lamb; but we never ask, what is the use of trying to realize their incomprehensible glories. We feel it to be both our duty and interest, to try what can be made of them, by meditation and prayer. We confess and rejoice, that the divine character sometimes opens on the mind, in such light and loveliness, such power and glory, that we are amply repaid for all the time, and thought, and prayer, which led to these discoveries. We know, that still brighter discoveries would be the certain reward of a more devotional spirit. We have told our souls, on retiring from some secret interviews with God, that they were for ever without excuse, if ever they doubted the fact or the felicity of communion with God, or ever grudged the time required for it. Even these passing hints awaken recollections of times of refreshing from the presence of the Lord, which compel us to exclaim, "O, that it were with me as in months past, when the secret of God was upon my tabernacle, and his candle shined on my head." Let, therefore, these experimental facts answer the question,—what is the use of trying to comprehend the incomprehensible?

Besides, what is it, in eternal glory, that is so very incomprehensible? We ourselves have not spent so very much time or thought upon the subject, as warrants us to pronounce it inconceivable; and the books written upon it, are neither so many nor so meagre as to prove that little can be made of it. Baxter's Saints' Everlasting Rest, and especially his Dying Thoughts, are not failures. Drexelius was too ignorant of the gospel to succeed; and Cayley too quaint; and Welwood too fanciful. Besides, like the present little work, all these books are too small to determine the real capabilities of the subject. They only prove, when compared with our standard works on other lofty topics, how little has ever been attempted on this one. Is it not evident, that if we had nothing more elaborate and profound on the subject of the divine character and government; of the glory and grace of the atonement; of the nature and effects of divine influence; there would be less interest taken in these cardinal points than there now is? Can any thoughtful man doubt, that, if Baxter's time and thought had been equally divided between eternity and controversy; Owen's, between it and doctrine; Howe's, between it and discussion; Doddridge's, between it and experience; Jeremy Taylor's, between it and casuistry; we should have had works on Eternity, as valuable and sublime as the other master-pieces of these master-spirits? They would, of course, have all failed to define everlasting duration, and to specify the precise character of the "fullness" of heavenly engagements or enjoyments. What then? A *definition* of eternity would not be of much use, if we had one; and, therefore, the impossibility of grasping the idea of never-ending duration, is a poor apology for not trying to realize eternal things. The mental effort of measuring "everlasting" is not the exercise we are called to engage in; nor is it one that could lead to any spiritual result, even if we were qualified to make that effort.

In like manner, the usual objections founded upon the general character of invisible things, are more plausible than weighty. For, what if we cannot *map* out the landscape of heaven? We know that it is "Emmanuel's land," our "Father's house," the temple and the throne of "God and the Lamb." There is surely enough in all this both to instruct and delight, however little we can make of its sea of glass or its river of life. What if we ought not to attach material ideas to its crowns, or palms, or harps? They are tokens of divine favor, and of the joy that springs from that favor; and these are ideas equally simple and sublime. What if we can form no idea of the precise *order* in which the "general assembly" are arranged around the throne? They are around the throne where Deity reigns in unveiled glory!—a fact so distinct and transporting, that the mind which will dwell on it for a moment, will feel incapable of giving a thought to the childish question of local arrangements. The armies of heaven are in the immediate presence of *" the God of order."* That is enough. What, also, if we can form no idea of the precise way in which angels and the redeemed interchange their knowledge, and reciprocate their enjoyments, nor of the way in which God and the Lamb communicate their will and feelings to both ? There is communion between saints and angels, and between the Godhead and both. And, as it must be in a way *worthy* of the majesty of the divine nature and character, and becoming the intelligence of perfect spirits, questions about speech or language are really unworthy of such a subject. For, could we answer them, the knowledge of the forms and mediums of mental communication, could add little to the grandeur of the fact, that there is communion with God and with each other. What, also, if we can neither tell nor conceive, whether all things in heaven and throughout the universe will remain for ever, exactly as they will subsist at the consummation of time; or whether the cycles of eternity will witness the creation of new worlds, and new orders of beings, and the establishment amongst them of new systems of moral probation? We know what is better,—that God will "*rest in his love*" to all the redeemed. No event will ever occur to alienate his heart, or hide his face, or divert his attention from them. Whatever new creations may arise in the universe, they will not displace the church from her rank in his esteem. Whatever order of angels or worlds may outstrip the rest in the career of improvement, they will never eclipse her; yea, whatever possible modification of moral government may be introduced into any possible creation, the *mediatorial,* under which the church of Christ was formed and perfected, will remain eternally the glory of the divine administration. "We shall be for ever with the Lord," whatever other beings may be brought into existence; and for ever *nearest* to him, whatever new relations he may sustain to new worlds. He will die no more, he lives for ever, and, therefore, they must be for ever dearest to him, for whom he shed his blood.

There may be no events of this kind to diversify the ages and bliss of eternity. The supposition of them is not, however, rash nor improbable. And one thing is certain, if variety ever be wanted in order to perpetuate or promote the happiness of heaven, there is space enough in infinity for all the worlds and systems which omnipotence can create, should every age of eternity be marked by a new creation as vast as the old.

But to close this series of questions,—what if we cannot now realize either the precise kind or degree of our *knowledge* in heaven. We are sure that it will be satisfactory, both in kind and degree. It will impart and prolong "fullness of joy;"—and what more could we wish? We naturally advert, when we think of heavenly knowledge, to the mystery of the divine essence; and wonder whether we shall understand the unity of the Trinity. Few, perhaps, have felt more curiosity on this point than myself. I have so often dwelt upon this question, that I am actually ashamed of the degree in which it has occupied my attention. For, however desirable or pleasing it might be to understand this mystery, it is self-evident when we pause to reflect, that even the perfect knowledge of it could not add much to our enjoyment. It would rather gratify our curiosity than increase our happiness. Indeed, its moral bearings upon present or future bliss are any thing but obvious. Not that I am indifferent to such knowledge, nor underrate it; but when I ask myself, how it would profit me,

I must say that I cannot answer the question. I cannot but see, that even if I understood all mysteries, and *this* one most, I should still have to find my happiness in the *character* of God. The comprehension of his essence, however full and clear, could not answer the same moral purposes as the comprehension of his love, his wisdom, or his faithfulness. And as there is no doubt but these will be known and enjoyed in perfection, I must say to myself and to others, that we should sustain no spiritual loss were this mystery to be as eternal as it is now entire.

I do not, however, think that it will be so. The assurance that "we shall know, even as we are known," pledges, if not open vision on the subject, such a degree of light as shall render the union of Father, Son, and Spirit, in the one Godhead, as obvious as the union of soul, body, and spirit in our own one person. But as it will not be from knowing the points where the latter blend, nor the nexus of their unity, but from the intellectual and moral powers thus produced and perfected; so, whatever be the light thrown upon the unity of the Trinity, our chief confidence and delight in the Godhead must spring from its moral perfections, and not from its physical properties. In a word,—we shall know all that finite intellect can enjoy or bear; and, surely, there is range enough in that wide and warm circle of light, to render the anticipation of the perfect day of eternity equally pleasing and profitable.

Thus there is really less difficulty in conceiving of invisible things, than appears at first sight. The current objections against trying to realize them are not so formidable as they are plausible. They are, in fact, rather the suggestions of *sloth*, than the convictions of reason; and far less derived from baffled effort to comprehend, than from reluctance to meditate.

I must now say distinctly, that I have a very mean opinion of all the ordinary excuses, put forward to palliate or explain the slight attention given to eternal things. I feel thus, especially, in reference to the wrath to come. When that is dwindled into a question about the *materiality* of everlasting burnings, both the head and the heart do themselves little credit. For, whatever unquenchable fire, or the deathless worm, may literally mean, they can mean nothing good,—nothing easy,—nothing temporary. Besides, to a mind rightly exercised and disposed, there is surely more than enough to awe it, and to fix its awe, in the single fact, that hell is "the wrath of God and the Lamb." There can be no great soundness of judgment nor justness of feeling, where the impression of this solemn fact is defeated or weakened by curiosity. It does, therefore, appear to me one of the deceits of the human heart, if not one of the wiles of Satan, when our thoughts entangle themselves with the minute details of future misery, and thus escape from the awful and obvious truth, that it is "everlasting destruction from the presence of the Lord, and from the glory of his power." Yes; hell is this, whatever else it is, and whatever else it is not. Of what consequence then is the question, what else is hell, seeing it is *this?* O, did we estimate things according to their real or their relative importance, there is in this one view of the wrath to come, such definite and appalling terrors, that even a momentary glance at them, if given daily, could not fail to keep us fleeing from that wrath, and clinging with a death-grasp to the cross, as the only refuge from it.

No. III.

THE EXCUSES FOR NOT REALIZING ETERNITY.

However natural it may be to prefer the prospect of immortality to the horrid idea of annihilation, it is certainly neither natural nor common to think often of immortality. It is not so attractive to us as annihilation is repulsive. We dislike the bare idea of coming to such an end as "the beasts which perish;" but we do not, proportionably, *love* the bright hope of being "as the angels of God in heaven." We do not turn to the latter with the promptness or spirit that we turn away from the former. Indeed, our reluctance to speak or think much of immortality is almost as great as our aversion to annihilation. This is a strange inconsistency! We loathe the extinction of our being, and yet shrink from dwelling on the eternity of it. This would be very inconsistent, even if the gospel did no more than proclaim redemption from the hell it reveals, without at all describing the heaven it promises. Mere escape from everlasting misery, to eternal life of any other kind, and in any other place, would deserve more consideration than we usually give to our "Father's house." O, yes; were we never to see God as he is, nor the Lamb in his essential glory; never to see the throne nor the temple of Deity; never to behold one angel, nor to hear one anthem of the heaven of heavens; even the bare prospect of not being under the *wrath* of God and the Lamb, would be worth more attention and gratitude than we commonly pay to the full-orbed prospect of being for ever with the Lord, and with all who are the Lord's. Indeed, if the gospel were utterly silent on the subject of heaven, and said nothing else to commend or enforce its own claims, but just that, by believing and obeying it, we should escape the abode of "the devil and his angels," it would be glad tidings of great joy, and worthy of all acceptation. But this is not the gospel, nor yet like it. It opens heaven as fully as it uncovers hell. It says quite as much to render heaven alluring, as to render hell alarming.

It is not, therefore, owing to any defect in

bliss or glory, nor to any deficiency of information concerning them, that we meditate so seldom and slightly upon them. The Old Testament saints, who knew far less of these eternal realities than we do, realized them far more than we do. This is no gratuitous compliment to their heavenly-mindedness. God, who cannot lie nor err, has expressly testified that their life and conversation " declare plainly" that they *desired* "a heavenly country," and "looked for a city which hath foundations, whose builder and maker is God." Why is it, then, that, in general, we are reluctant to dwell upon the prospects of a glorious immortality; and that we require to plan, and watch, and pray, and resolve, before we can at all enter into the spirit of heavenly contemplation; and, that we do not always succeed, even when we make an effort to pass within the veil? It is very pitiful when this question is answered by the cold remark, " We know too little of heaven to think much about it. We rather know what it is not, than what it is. It is chiefly described by *negatives.*" Negatives! True; but they are glorious negatives. No night! no death! no sin! no suffering or sorrow! This is what heaven is not. And is all this too little to furnish matter for frequent and profound meditation? Sin cannot be a very oppressive burden to the mind that takes no pleasure in contemplating eternal freedom from the very *being*, as well as from the love and power of sin. Ignorance, and liability to mistake and err, cannot be very irksome to the mind that is not delighted with the prospect of seeing "face to face" all the things which we "now see through a glass darkly." Pain and death cannot be much felt or feared, nor the vicissitudes of life much reckoned on, where the prospect of "no more curse" has little or no attraction. It is, therefore, very pitiful, when the negatives of revelation are appealed to, as reasons for not looking much to the things which are unseen and eternal. Were any of the lowest of these negatives to become true of any place in this world, that place would soon be attractive and popular. The discovery of a country in which there was no pain, or no sickness, would be a theme of enthusiastic congratulation. Such a place would soon be crowded; and even those who staid at home would be unable to forbear from thinking of it, although it were described only by negatives. Such a negative as "no suffering," would be held to be a positive good, and be hailed with general gratitude. And, as heaven is the entire and eternal *negation* of all evil, natural and moral, they evince little mind, and less conscience, who excuse their inattention to it by the pretence, "that we know what it is not, rather than what it is."

It is also common to put forward a better excuse in a worse form; because an unscriptural form. How often are both speaking and thinking, abruptly broken off, by quoting the words of Paul, "Eye hath not seen, nor ear heard, neither have entered into the heart of man, the things which God hath prepared for them that love him." This too is pitiful, whether it arise from ignorance or inattention; for Paul immediately adds, "But God hath revealed them unto us by his Spirit." 1 Cor. ii. 9, 10. This the apostle repeats with triumph; "Now we have received not the spirit of the world, but the Spirit which is of God, that we *might know the things which are freely given us of God;* which things also we speak." So far, therefore, is the apostolic argument from being an apology for not attempting to realize heaven, that it is, in fact and intention, a strong reason for looking much and often to the joy set before us. Well might BAXTER say, "Think on the joys above as boldly as Scripture hath expressed them. To conceive of glory, only as above our conception, will beget little love; or, as above our love, will produce little joy." Baxter, indeed, knew well, and Paul knew perfectly, that "the things which God hath prepared for them that love him" surpass all knowledge and comprehension: but they knew, also, that God had revealed these things as freely and fully as they were utterable by words, or could be made intelligible by images; which is just as far as a *revelation* of them could go; and, therefore, these holy men found in this, inspiring reasons for frequent and rapturous contemplation of the saints' everlasting rest.

This case is similar to that of the love of Christ. It "passeth knowledge" in its breadth and length, its depth and height; but that is not held to be a valid reason for not trying to "comprehend" it. Accordingly, when we do try, we do comprehend enough of its "breadth," to see *room* for ourselves; enough of its "length," to see *residence* for ourselves; enough of its "depth," to see *support* for ourselves; enough of its "height," to see *security* for ourselves. Or, if at any time, or even often, we fail to see all this in the dimensions and duration of the love of Christ, we feel that the failure is owing to our own blindness or unbelief, and not to any defect in His love. Besides, its incomprehensibleness is felt to be a part of its glory. We understand and enjoy it most when we are constrained to say, "It passeth knowledge!" When Paul uttered this exclamation, and its emphatic accompaniments, he saw more of the wonders of redeeming love than he had ever seen before. His mind was *out* amongst its immeasurable glories, as Newton's was abroad in the universe, when he said it was unsearchable. This, in Newton's lips, was not the language of ignorance, nor of disappointment. He saw the distant and dazzling points at which the universe *became* unsearchable; and never knew nor enjoyed so much, as when he thus felt, through all his soul, that it "passeth knowledge." In like manner, Paul saw the *point* of breadth, the *point* of length, the *point* of depth, the *point* of height, at which the love of Christ, like the spaces of infinity, surpasseth comprehension.

So it is with the glories of heaven. Enough may be discovered, by devotional meditation, to fill the heart with a "joy full of glory;" and that joy will *overflow* whenever it is really "unspeakable." There is, therefore, no such lack or indefiniteness of information, as would excuse inattention, or as should discourage effort. Behold, in revelation, "a ladder set up on earth," and the top thereof reacheth "to heaven;" and we, though not angels, may ascend and descend on it with perfect safety and daily advantage. It was not on this ladder that the Mystics ascended.

Is it, then, because we deem it *unnecessary* to our safety or comfort, that we set apart so little time for heavenly meditation? Are we influenced in this by the conduct of others; and, because so few seem heavenly minded, until they are dying, do we think it enough to be neighbor-like? Do we ever, to avoid the trouble of retiring to meditate on heaven, try to prove that it is not necessary unto salvation to be heavenly minded? Are we rather pleased with, than ashamed of, the bald logic which could make it quite plausible, that a man may get to heaven at last, without thinking much about it by the way? Are we at all inclined to play off any of the doctrines of grace against the necessity of setting our affections on "things above?"

These questions are not so numerous or varied, as the ways in which the human heart tries to evade the claims of God and eternity upon its affections. It can play both dextrous and desperate games of hazard, when it is unwilling to yield to divine authority. Some persuade themselves that there is no hazard even in allowing an immoral habit of life to stand out against the law of God. Now, this *we* durst not allow in ourselves. This we brand with the deserved and disgraceful name of Antinomianism; the mark of the modern " beast and false prophet," whether blazoned on the " forehead," or hid in the " hand." There are, however, " lusts of the mind," as well as lusts of the flesh; and the desire to reserve the great bulk of our spare time for thinking and speaking of earthly things, is one of these mental lusts. The desire to have things right between God and the conscience, without the trouble of *keeping* them right, is another. Impatience to quit the closet is a third. Drawing in, or checking, those lines of thought which lead direct to eternity, is a fourth. Now, although none of these lusts of the mind amount to Antinomianism, there is enough of sin in them to make a conscientious man afraid and ashamed of them. We, therefore, ought not to parley with the mean questions, how little heavenly meditation is compatible with not risking heaven ; or, how much may we " mind earthly things," without missing eternal things at last ? These are calculations which the Searcher of hearts must despise, as dishonorable to Himself, and as discreditable to those who are bound to *please* Him. For how can we please Him, if we take little or no pleasure in the eternal weight of glory, which he has prepared for, and revealed to, them that love him?

Consider, we profess to have "like precious faith" with them who first loved God. Now, they could say, " Our conversation is in heaven." Their apostolic teachers could say of them, " Ye took joyfully the spoiling of your goods; knowing, in yourselves, that ye have in heaven a better and an enduring inheritance." Now, as we allow, and even try to make, our faith go all the length that their's went, in relying on the Saviour, and in depending on the Holy Spirit, and in following practical holiness, why not allow and employ it to be "the substance of things hoped, and the evidence of things not seen?" Hear how God appeals to us on behalf of this duty: " If ye be then risen with Christ, seek those things which are from above, where Christ sitteth at the right hand of God. Set your affections on things above, not on things on the earth." This spiritual command is as authoritative as the moral command annexed to it,—" Mortify your members which are upon the earth," (Col. i. 1—5.) Now, this moral command, so far as it regards the lusts of the flesh, we revere and obey. It is written upon our hearts as with the pen of a diamond. We deprecate and loathe any sophistry that would relax its authority over us, or soften the aspect of incontinence. This is as it should be; but why should the spiritual command be less heeded, or the neglect of it be less feared? It rests upon the same high authority, and is equally explicit. Its *sanction*, also, although it do not sound so awfully, is not less solemn than that of the former. The Saviour enforces heavenly-mindedness thus: " for where your treasure is, there will your hearts be also:" a consideration not less awful, when duly weighed, than the " wrath" threatened against the unclean; for if the " heart" be set on earthly things, the issue will be fatal to the soul.

It is easy to say, and to prove by words, that there is no comparison between sensuality and earthly-mindedness, in point of guilt. This is quite true, in more senses than one. It is, however, equally true, that there is much comparison between them in point of *tendency*. Accordingly, worldliness ruins quite as many as profligacy, if not more. It is equally powerful, and more plausible, in diverting the mind from God. It leaves as little room or relish in the heart for secret devotion, as vice can do. The sensualist is afraid to be *alone* with God; and the worldling grudges the time and dislikes the duty. In a word; as it is expressly declared that the sensual have not "the Spirit," so it is, that "if any man love the world, the love of the Father is not in him."

It is not intended by these remarks to confound even a low degree of heavenly-mindedness, with *this* love of the world. The former may co-exist with both the love and the fear of God for a time. A renewed mind is not a heavenly mind at once, nor always soon; but whilst this is readily granted, it is not less true, that a renewed mind can only *prove* its renewal to itself, by trying to set its affections on things above, as soon as the necessity of doing so is proved to be imperative; for to give ourselves full credit for being "born of God," whilst conscious of a wilful outstand against this divine command, would be both imprudent and presumptuous. Something must be, and *will* be done, in this matter, by an honest convert, that he may have a good conscience towards God in heavenly things, as well as towards man in earthly things. Much will not be done, however, until he is as fully persuaded of the *advantage*, as of the necessity of heavenly-mindedness; for where it is to begin, after we have gone on pretty well for years without it, it is not easy to see the use or the benefit of it. Indeed, at first sight, there seems more advantage to be derived from cultivating the *practical* virtues more carefully, than from thinking often about heaven. And there is much weight in the question,—Is not practical godliness the best preparation for heaven? The man who denies or doubts this, does not understand the design of the gospel. "The grace of God that bringeth salvation," bringeth it, "teaching us, that, denying all ungodliness and worldly lusts, we should live soberly, righteously, and godly, in this present world." But this is not all that it teaches us: all this is to be done, Paul says, "*looking* for that blessed hope, and the glorious appearing of the great God and our Saviour Jesus Christ," (Titus ii. 13.) Looking heavenward is, therefore, as much one of the lessons which grace teacheth, as looking well to our moral conduct, is another; and a *habit* of both is equally taught in the gospel. Accordingly, they will be found, on due examination, to be mutually necessary and useful to each other. Indeed, there can be no heavenly-mindedness, where there is little practical godliness. The man who is not both sober and honest, is unable to realize eternal things, so as to derive any enjoyment from them. There is a flaming sword between him, and "the tree of life, which is in the midst of the Paradise of God." It is quite unnecessary to caution him against devoting too much of his time or thought to the contemplation of future glory. His thoughts run in the opposite direction, when they are forced in amongst invisible realities.

On the other hand, however, it is equally true, that, without "looking for the blessed hope" of eternal life, there will be no eminent godliness. There may, indeed, be honesty, and sobriety, and benevolence, maintained, without much distinct reference to heaven; because these duties bring a daily reward, by increasing the comfortableness of the comforts of life. There are, however, duties, and those of equal importance too, which cannot be well discharged without a considerable degree of heavenly-mindedness, because their rewards are remote. The *religious* education of a family is one of these duties. Parents, who are content to let recollections of eternity come and go as may happen, and who take no pains to keep the light of eternity upon their domestic responsibilities, will neither do nor care much for the spiritual welfare of their children; but will also content themselves with the negative virtue of not setting a bad example before their offspring, and with the *cheap* discipline of an angry reproof, or a hasty punishment. In such families, also, nothing will be done to make *servants* wise unto salvation, except allowing or requiring them to attend public worship once on the Lord's-day. In like manner, where there is no habitual sense of unseen realities kept up, there will be no habitual effort to glorify God, by trying to do good to the souls of the poor and the perishing. Relief may be *sent* to the poor, and visiting societies supported for the spiritual benefit of the sick; but *personal* exertions to win souls will not be made, by any one whose personal piety has but little daily reference to eternity.

Nor are these the only duties which cannot be well discharged without some heavenly-mindedness. The Scriptures will not be much, nor very devotionally, searched, if we lose sight of the "eternal life" which they reveal. Secret prayer will not be very solemn nor constant, if we confine our attention to our *immediate* spiritual wants; for whatever truth there may be in the religious proverb, (and there is much,) that "dying grace is for a dying hour," it is equally true, that if grace to live well is not sought with an express reference to dying well, it will not be earnestly nor often sought. He will pray most in secret, and with most pleasure, whose closet is, as it were, a little *nook* of the heaven of heavens, partitioned off for communion with God, and whose times of retirement are regarded as portions of eternity. And there is special need, that the family altar should actually lean on the eternal throne; there is such danger of becoming formal and dull in domestic worship!

The advantages of heavenly-mindedness are not, however, confined to the duties of godliness: they extend also to religious *enjoyments*. Now, a "good hope through grace," is an enjoyment which we prize highly, and pray much for; because we find that we cannot go on well without it. We feel with Paul, that hope is the very "anchor of the soul." We call it emphatically, "*our sheet anchor;*" nor is there any impropriety in thus strengthening our sense of its importance, by the best form of its consecrated image. It would, however, be better to familiarize ourselves with the scriptural use of this fine image. Now,

REALIZING ETERNITY. 61

Paul says, that the anchor of hope *"entereth into* THAT *within the veil;* whither the forerunner is for us entered, even Jesus." "That within the veil," is evidently heaven. It is, therefore, when hope (like an anchor passing through the veil of the waters until it lay hold upon the channels of the waters) passes into heaven, that it becomes an anchor of the soul, "sure and steadfast," and thus furnishes "strong consolation." (Heb. vi. 19, 20.) If, therefore, we would enjoy or maintain a good hope through grace, we must make it to enter within the veil, not only when our souls are tempest-tossed, but also when there is "a great calm." Indeed, we shall not be able to use it as an anchor, in the storm, if we do not use it in the calm. Accordingly, those who use it rather as *ballast* to their character, than as an anchor of the soul, find, in the hour of temptation and trial, that they cannot cast it within the veil. They try; but it will not take hold of " THAT " which is within. Their hope drags, like an anchor on bad moorings. Not, indeed, that using it as ballast to the character, is the cause of this. Hope should, yea, must, be employed to steady the life, as well as to cheer the heart. It will, however, be unable to enter within the veil, whilst all without the veil is dark and threatening, if it do not accustom itself to enter when all without is tranquil. Our souls must send hope heavenward, even when they *least* need the consolation, if they would stand prepared to enjoy that consolation when they *most* need it.

The spirit, although not the form, of these hints, is equally applicable to the enjoyment of *peace* of conscience. This, also, is very dear, and justly so, to all true believers; and, like every other spiritual joy, it has both its source and centre in the Cross of Christ. But whilst it was the blood of Christ that made peace, and whilst it is faith in that blood which brings peace into the conscience, it is heaven which tests *our* peace in believing, and shows " what sort it is : " for if it will not bear to be confronted with heaven, it is not such a peace as the atonement is calculated to afford ; and, therefore, not such as should satisfy us. Nothing, however, is farther from my intention, in these remarks, than to insinuate that there is *no* faith in the atonement, when there is no assurance of eternal life, or whilst heaven is not directly contemplated. There is much evidence of true faith, when a conscience, once burthened with guilt, and agitated with fear, is so tranquillized by scriptural views of the cross, that the believer is both able and willing to engage in all the ordinary duties of life with composure and determination. This is as truly "the work of faith," and as properly so, as any effort to set our affections on things above : for we belong to time as well as to eternity; to this world, as well as to that which is to come ; and are, therefore, equally bound to discharge the duties of both. It would, therefore, be decidedly wrong to form a habit of so contemplating heaven, as if we were just about to leave the world. This is not what is wanted. It is, however, necessary, as we know not when we must leave the world, that our faith should often try how our peace will stand the test of a steady look at heaven. Let it, by all means, look at the duties of life and godliness; and observe well, how it is affected by them ; and let all its holy influence upon them be set down as proof of its being "the peace of God," which springs from faith in Christ. It must not, however, be allowed to stop here. Our peace must be frequently confronted with heaven also, if we would have it to "keep our hearts and minds" truly happy. For, as there must be something wrong or defective in it, if thinking of eternity disturbs it; so our own consciousness of this disturbance must create a suspicion that we may have no peace, when we are *compelled* to think of eternity: for if the prospect agitate us, how must the reality overpower us on our death-bed? Whereas, by seeking from day to day, a peace which shall "reign unto eternal life," as well as sweeten our temporal life, we shall do best for both worlds.

It is now easy to see how heavenly-mindedness must maintain and promote *love* to the Saviour. We often lament the coldness and deadness of our hearts towards Him. There are few prayers that we utter so fervently, as that of WATTS:

> "Come, Holy Spirit, heavenly Dove,
> With all thy quickening powers;
> Come, shed abroad a Saviour's love,
> And that shall kindle ours!"

Well, the Spirit we thus invoke, works by means. He quickens by *quickening motives;* and one of them is, the hope of glory. Now, this he employs so much for kindling love to Christ, that one of his own titles is, "the earnest of the inheritance" in heaven. By trying, therefore, to set our affections on things above, we are taking the most natural way, and the most spiritual too, of setting them upon the Saviour himself. Indeed, it is impossible to love him as we ought, or even as we might, without contemplating frequently both the wrath to come, from which He delivers; and the glory to come, which He has prepared.

No. IV.

NOMINAL FAITH, FROM NOT REALIZING ETERNITY.

What ought believers, and especially ministers, to think of that *national faith* which Christianity has obtained in this country? Any zealot can despise it; and any theorist expose its defects. Both, however, would be startled, were the national faith transferred from Protestantism to Popery, or to Deism, or even to Socinianism. Such an apostasy would be appalling, even to those who brand popular faith, as absolute unbelief. They would be the first to proclaim its guilt, and to predict its punishment. National faith is not, therefore, a worthless nor a useless thing. Even nominal Christianity is infinitely preferable to real infidelity. The latter would throw back the moral character of the country, and render salvation impossible; whereas the former, with all its awful defects,—and they are as enormous as numerous,—maintains many virtues, and helps to keep the golden candlestick of the gospel in Britain.

Is there, then, no faith at all in this popular belief? However this may be, there is as much truth passed into currency, as keeps popular feeling hostile to Popery and Socinianism. Public opinion is against the great heresies, both of ancient and modern times. Indeed, except in a few obscure places, it is impossible for any minister to speak more highly of the glory or the grace of the Saviour, than the public mind would bear. Neither the "Amen," nor the "Alleluia," of the people would be withheld from the loftiest form of his worship.

Such being the sober and familiar facts of the case, that man's orthodoxy ought not to be suspected, who ventures to doubt the wisdom of *despising* and *denouncing* national faith. He ought, at least, to obtain a fair hearing, even when he hazards the assertion, that *exposures* of its defects and fallacies are not the only nor the best means of removing them. It is as easy, as it is true, to tell nominal believers, that they do not understand nor love the gospel which they profess to believe;

that they have no spiritual discernment of its glory, and no humbling sense of their need of its grace. This, alas, is the fact; but the question is, why is this the case? It is easy to say, because they do not seek to be taught by the Spirit of God. This also is only too true! But here, also, the question, "Why is this the case," is necessary. Why are the generality so insensible of their need of divine teaching, and so averse to pray for it? Here, again, it is as easy, as it is true, to say, that they love the world so much, and sin so well, that "the things of the Spirit are foolishness" to them. Still the question returns, why do they so love the world and sin? Now, when we say that such is human nature, whilst *unregenerate*, we ought to remember, that such was our nature, and that of all believers, before conversion. What, therefore, was the grand consideration which the eternal Spirit employed for changing our *nominal* belief of the gospel, into *cordial* faith? What gave that force to truth; and that effect to trials; and that power to conscience; and that aspect to sin; which arrested our unbelief, and decided our character? The Christian, who will examine this matter duly in his own case, will find that it was the weight of eternity which turned the scale. And if he will pass from his own case, to that of the first Christians, he will find, in a more remarkable degree, that it was by motives drawn from all the heights and depths of eternity, that the Holy Spirit won faith to the cross.

Now, if this be the historical and experimental fact, is it not both self-evident and certain, that nominal belief must prevail, until eternity is brought to bear more fully and frequently on the public mind? Are we wiser than Christ and the apostles, that we deal so much in exposures of defect and fallacy in nominal faith, and so little in manifestations of eternal things? Are we so ignorant of human nature, as to imagine that the way to set men right, is to prove that they are wrong? Unmasking and analyzing character, principle, and motives, formed, indeed, a special part of the Saviour's ministry. He never met the scribes or the pharisees, without exposing both their hypocrisy and self-righteousness. But, whilst this is true, it is equally true that all this was done in direct connection with eternity. Their hypocrisy was laid open and lashed, not chiefly by contrasting it with the *sincerity* of the pious, but by kindling upon it " the damnation of hell." Their boasting righteousness was weighed, and found wanting; but not in the scales of comparison only, nor in the scales of law chiefly, but in those of judgment and eternity. Every thing was brought to an eternal issue, and kept in the full blaze of heaven's glories, or of hell's flames. Thus the Saviour gave the scribes and pharisees something more to do, than to mark how their spirit differed from that of the penitent and the humble; He made them notice and feel, how it differed from all that constitutes meetness for heaven, and how it breathed "the savor of death unto death."

This characteristic of the Saviour's ministry may be traced in all his sermons to all classes. Everlasting life, or everlasting misery, is always the great motive by which he enforces every duty; and the *only* motive by which he enforces faith. Indeed, it might have been with an express reference to the mere *moral reasonings* of the present day, and as a standing protest against them, that he ran all his lessons into eternity. When he argues against a besetting sin, he spends no time in proving its baneful influence upon personal or domestic happiness; but appeals, at once, to the final result of indulgence, "everlasting fire." Matt. xviii. 8, 9. In like manner, when he enforces mutual forgiveness and forbearance on his disciples, no time is lost in shifting these duties through all the signs of the zodiac of propriety; but an unforgiving servant is placed at once in the hands of "the tormentors," and the disciples told, "So likewise shall my heavenly Father do also unto you, if ye from your hearts forgive not every one his brother their trespasses." If it is only the calling of opprobrious names, he approaches the sin without any circumlocution, and says, "Whosoever shall say, thou fool, shall be in danger of hell fire." If it is but *one* member of the body that requires to be mortified, he threatens the "whole body" with hell, unless that member be crucified. "This is not the manner of man, O Lord God!" It was, however, the Saviour's manner of enforcing faith and obedience; and the effect of it was—the prevention of *nominal* belief, or the speedy detection of nominal believers. Under the ministry of Christ, men had to believe for eternity, or not at all ; for he kept all truth and duty for ever upon the battlements of heaven, or upon the brink of hell. So did his apostles. The first and the final appeals of both, on behalf of faith and repentance, were, invariably and directly, to "the powers of the world to come."

The consequence was, as has been already stated, that nominal faith did not prevail then. It had no leader to rally under. There was no apostle of the Lamb afraid to mention hell

"To ears polite."

Those who said, "I am of Paul, and I am of Apollos," did not avow this preference, because of any difference of doctrine or spirit between these preachers, on the subject of the wrath to come. Both, "knowing the terrors of the Lord, persuaded men," and wielded these terrors with equal frequency and fidelity. Neither of them was an "awful preacher," in the sense of being—unfeeling, or clamorous in proclaiming the wrath to come. They had weighed that wrath too deeply, and they believed it too firmly, to brawl or rave when they denounced or described it. They did, however, both describe and denounce it. It was not hushed up, nor hurried over, in their sermons. It was not, indeed, *dwelt* upon, nor unnecessarily dragged into their sermons; but, when it was brought unto them, it came as "the wrath of God and the Lamb;"—a solemn, settled, and eternal reality! Those who heard Paul say, "Indignation and wrath, tribulation and anguish, on every soul of man that doeth evil," durst not have said that Paul was in a *passion*. However any one shrunk or shuddered, no one could calm his fears by charging the apostle with heat or harshness, when he exclaimed, " The Lord Jesus shall be revealed from heaven with his mighty angels, in flaming fire, taking vengeance on them that know not God, and obey not the gospel of our Lord Jesus Christ." This, if even uttered in thunder, outspake, like the Sinai trumpet, all the thunder, and outshone all the lightning, of voice or visage, which could accompany it. It might be braved by the reckless, and disbelieved by the skeptical; but it could not be evaded nor evaporated, by those who trembled, by the stale pretence of undue warmth or savage ferocity. It is as much too solemn to be passion, as is the thunder of the heavens to be noise. This description of the coming of Christ, to punish " with everlasting destruction," must have been uttered almost as solemnly as if Paul, in the presence of it, had said, " Behold, he cometh."

Now, of this manner and spirit of preaching " eternal judgment," there is by far too little in the present day; and the prevalence of nominal faith is the proof and the effect of the deficiency. Men could not remain at "ease in Zion," in such numbers, and so long, if the terrors of the Lord were rightly used " to persuade men." They may be often and awfully employed to terrify men; and yet produce no effect, or only a bad effect. Harsh denunciations of wrath are just as likely to harden the conscience, as silence on the subject of hell is to lull conscience asleep. Accordingly, it is no uncommon thing to find hell least feared where it is most familiar. This is only what might be expected. The terrors of the Lord, if not used for persuasion, and in a persuasive spirit, will be resented or ridiculed. The gospel, however, can neither be preached nor believed without the use of them. It is not the "great salvation" that is proclaimed, when heaven only is opened and offered. That is, also, a salvation from hell; and, therefore, it is compromised and misrepresented, whenever the wrath to come is less exhibited than the glory to be revealed. It is even *defeated*, when that wrath is reluctantly, or hesitatingly, or but slightly hinted at; for any appearance of faltering or fearing, in the proclamation of it, hinders the belief of it; and thus prevents the belief of the gospel. For no man does or can believe the gospel, until he believe that he is in danger of perishing eternally. Now, although the frequent pressing home of that danger is not the best way of producing the belief of it, slight references to it are sure to prevent the fear of perishing; because their slightness is held to betray the same doubt or dislike, on the part of the speaker, as is felt by the hearers. They interpret the reluctance to touch the subject, and the haste to leave it, and the pain evinced while naming it, as signs of secret disbelief; or regard them as transcripts of their own suspicions and aversion. And, if they see that they are humored, and almost countenanced in their dislike of the subject, by the way in which it is hurried over, they will soon justify that dislike.

O, what wisdom! what prudence! is requisite, in order to preach the gospel. Christ is a Saviour from eternal misery, or not a Saviour at all; and yet nothing is so disbelieved as that misery. The very *silence* which is maintained on the subject of hell, proves how much it is disbelieved. The loudness and violence with which infidels deny and deride hell, betray more secret dread of it, than the silence of others indicates faith in it. The generality are silent, because they secretly hope or wish it to be untrue. They could not keep their thoughts or their lips so habitually clear of the subject, if it were not deeply doubted. The very hypocrites in Zion could not be silent if they believed in "everlasting burnings."

How ought this prevalent unbelief to be treated? is a question of immense importance. It admits, however, of a very simple answer, if Scripture, and not vain philosophy, be consulted. "The wrath to come" must be *asserted* in the pulpit as it is in the Bible,—explicitly, solemnly, and persuasively; and never treated controversially. The Saviour never proves its truth or its justice by abstract reasonings. The apostles never demonstrate, by arguments, the certainty or the necessity of the hell they proclaim. Both assert it, as they do the being of God, in unequivocal and unqualified terms. They never recognize nor refer to any objection, aversion, doubt, or question, which any one might entertain on the subject. If there were, in their audiences, those who professed to find any thing in the divine character or government, with which hell is inconsistent; or any thing in the nature of human guilt, which renders it unjust; or any thing in the gospel, which disproves it; neither Christ nor his apostles ever paid such reasoners the compliment of reasoning with them. Both unbelievers and doubters, on other subjects, were often and anxiously argued with. The Saviour went particularly and fully into any detail, or any line of argument, in order to prove to gainsayers his Messiahship and Sonship. And the apostles not only met all the popular objections and prejudices against the doctrines of grace, but seem even to have anticipated the more *profound* evasions of future times; that, thus, they might "cut off occasion" from all who sought occasion for urging their feelings or their philosophy against the gospel of the grace of God. But not thus—never thus, do they treat the unbelief of the heart, or of the mind, on the subject of hell. Like heaven and God—it is left to speak for itself. As the sacred writers never prove, by reasoning, that there is a heaven, neither do they argue the fact of hell with any man. They no more think it necessary to prove that eternal misery is not too *bad* to be true, than that eternal glory is not too *good* to be true. The horrors of the former are no more allowed to bring its truth into debate or doubt, than the raptures of the latter are allowed to bring its reality into question. Both are placed and left on the single ground of *inspired assertion.* Both are amply described, but neither is ever discussed.

Now this is what is wanted. Ministers, and teachers, and parents, must say nothing of hell but what God has said; and that only in his own words, in general. Man is not equal to amplify the revelation of wrath. He is not to be trusted with optional freedom in depicting the horrors of a desolate eternity. He cannot keep his own wrath out of gratuitous descriptions of the wrath of God and the Lamb. Whenever, therefore, it is brought in as "a fiery stream," it should be self-evident that "the breath of Jehovah" hath kindled it. Whenever the "horrible tempest" is shown, it should be seen that HE rains "the snares, fire, and brimstone." Whenever a minister descends into the bottomless pit to describe it, he must manifest that he is no more in his *element* than was the "mighty angel" of the Apocalypse, who descended to bind Satan; and yet, like that angel, he must not flinch nor falter; but use as freely and honestly all that God has said, as the angel used the "great chain." The hell of the Bible, like the heaven of the Bible, needs no coloring, and admits of no softening.

It is, therefore equally pitiful when, in reference to future misery, one minister acquires the name of a *harsh* preacher, and another that of a *gentle* preacher. He is unwise, who attempts to terrify by other visions of hell than those which revelation presents; and he is worse than unwise, who is less ample or explicit than Christ was. It is shameful to plead the gentleness of Christ, or the mild genius of Christianity, as a warrant for touching, seldom or slightly, on the painful subject of " everlasting destruction." This is a mere pretence. Christ is the great preacher of the wrath to come. He spoke more frequently and more emphatically of it, than any or all the messengers of God. And the only mildness of the genius of the gospel, on this subject, is, the perfect freeness, fullness, and certainty of the salvation from that wrath, which it proffers and proclaims. It pretends to and warrants none of that *mildness*, which conceals or softens hell. It makes no provision, and no allowance, for the weakness of any man's nerves, or for the delicacy of his taste, or for the conjectures of his reason, except the provision for saving him from the reality of that hell, the prospect of which shocks him. The gospel provides amply for our safety from hell; but not at all to exempt us from believing the eternity of future punishment, or our own exposure to it. Indeed, the truth of that hell, and of our own danger, is the very basis or occasion of all the glad tidings of the gospel. They are glad tidings of great joy, just because Tophet is an eternal reality, and sin an infinite evil.

Let men know, therefore, what they are about, whilst debating, or doubting, or evading this point: they are both rejecting the gospel, and treating God as a liar. That gospel proceeds upon the very fact and principle, that the punishment of sin is "everlasting destruction from the presence of the Lord, and from the glory of his power." How, then, can it be believed, whilst this is disbelieved? Believing it in order to be made better, or in order to make sure of heaven, is very proper and necessary; but this is not enough. It is the gospel of deliverance from the wrath to come; and must, therefore, be believed for the sake of that deliverance. But for this, it is not, and cannot be believed, if the danger is questioned.

Here, then, is the real cause of nominal faith, and of its prevalence. Very few believe that they deserve, or have incurred, the wrath of God. The generality think, whatever they may say, that they do not deserve eternal punishment. Accordingly, the belief they give to the gospel, is given to it as a moral remedy; or as a true religion; or as an authenticated history. It is believed, just as if there were no hell; or as if sin did not lead to the place " prepared for the devil and his angels." In a word, the current credence it obtains in the nation, is not for the sake of what is the *first* purpose for which Christ died; which is, to " deliver from going down to the pit."

Here an important question arises :—how is this inveterate disbelief of danger to be vanquished? Now, I may safely assert, at once, that it never was vanquished in any mind, by abstract reasonings on the nature or the desert of sin. The cry, " Lord, save, I perish," was not won nor wrung from your own heart by the force of moral or legislative considerations. You are not a trophy nor a monument of the power of abstract truth. It is not, chiefly, because you see how sin affects the character and government of God, that you believe the certainty and the necessity of eternal punishment. Your former unbelief on this point was borne down, and is kept down, just by the solemn fact, that God has said that " the wicked shall be turned into hell, where the worm dieth not, and the fire is not quenched." It is the weight of His declarations, and not your own insight into the nature of things, or into the philosophy of moral government, that fixes your convictions of hell. Its revealed truth enables you to reason on its abstract justice; and all the character of the great atonement confirms your reasonings; but it was on the single and solemn ground of "Thus saith the Lord," that you began either to reason or believe. Your faith, in this matter, stands on the word of God, and not on the word of man, nor on your natural perceptions of the eternal fitness of things.

Now, what won you to flee from the wrath to come, and thus to believe on Christ for everlasting life, is just what is wanted in the case of all nominal believers. They cannot be argued nor enticed into the belief of their danger. No exposure of the defects of their faith, will remedy these defects. The wisdom of man is foolishness here, whenever it tries to drive or draw without considerations "full of immortality." We must have faith in the force of God's own words, on the subject of heaven and hell. They want no helping out from man. What is wanted, is, the full impression of them; the spiritual apprehension of them; the solemn realization of their truth and interest. Then, both the formal and the heartless must feel, that they are not believing the gospel, whilst they continue to disbelieve their own danger of perishing; and must see, that they are at open issue with God on a turning point in religion. Now, as even the most heedless would not give himself credit for any real faith in the gospel if he doubted and hated the doctrine of it concerning HEAVEN; his secret disbelief of his doctrine concerning HELL, may and ought to be publicly charged on him as proof of his unbelief.

No. V.

SPIRITUAL DECLENSION, FROM NOT REALIZING ETERNITY.

At first sight, it seems *surprising*, as well as deplorable, that we should ever sink into heartless formality in the worship of God, or into cold apathy under the Word of God; seeing his word is the only substitute we have for his presence, and his worship the chief emblem and prelude of heaven. And yet, there are times, and these, alas! too frequent, when we pray without fervency, and praise without gratitude, and hear without any lively interest. Truths which have made "our heart burn within us," can hardly fix our ear then; and songs and supplications which have been almost "unutterable," by their intensity, are scarcely worth uttering then, owing to their heartlessness. The words of prayer and praise are the same;

but the spirit and the life of them are gone. Even the natural *tones* have forsaken the terms of devotion. The very sound of honest and artless feeling is lost.

Now, we may well be ashamed of such declensions of the spirit of devotion: but, ought we to wonder at them? Is it really surprising that the power of godliness should thus evaporate, until the very form of it is ready to vanish away?

However this may be, we are surprised as well as sorry. We do wonder that truths and duties, which have often both interested and absorbed our whole soul, should ever become either tame or tedious, dim or dull, to us. We feel this especially, when they become so, even whilst we are not unholy nor untender in our general character or conduct; and when we cannot trace the unhappy change of feeling to any change of habits. We are conscious that a blight has fallen upon our spirit; but unconscious of bringing it on by any allowed misconduct. Our character is much the same, as when our spirit was lively and devotional: and, as we have not relinquished nor altered any of our religious principles, we are amazed, as well as grieved, that our hearts should become thus alienated from the power of religion.

In this dilemma it is not uncommon to have recourse to a false principle of explanation. Some ascribe the decay to the *sovereign* withdrawment of the Divine Presence; meaning by that, the hiding of God's countenance from the soul, as an *experiment* upon the soul. Others, justly afraid of resolving into absolute sovereignty, what is but too easily explained by the weakness of human nature, ascribe the decay to that weakness. They say, "it is only what might be expected in the case of imperfect creatures, whilst in a world so imperfect." Thus they lay their account with sinking into occasional deadness and formality; and regard the declension as a matter of course, or of inevitable necessity.

This solution is as unwise as the other is impious. Not, however, that there are no circumstances which upset the power of godliness for a time. There are: and, under them, the Christian is, perhaps, quite as much an object of pity as of blame. The shock of sudden calamity, or a severe prostration of strength and spirits, is almost sure to overpower, or impair, the spirituality of the mind. Neither devotional habits nor feelings, which have been formed in health and prosperity, can accommodate themselves, at once, to pain and poverty,

They are both shaken and shattered for a time. And, then, it is not improper nor imprudent to take the full comfort of the gracious assurance, that our pitying Father "knoweth our frame, and remembereth that we are dust."

It is not, however, safe nor wise to have recourse to this principle, when neither the body nor the mind is broken down by care. Any decay of spirituality that occurs, whilst we are in ordinary circumstances of character and condition, will be found to spring from inattention to ETERNITY.

This is a much more frequent and fruitful source of religious declension than we are apt to suspect, or willing to believe; because we forget or overlook the degree in which the light of eternity was upon divine things, when we were first and most affected by them. This is the real *secret* of those relapses, which we cannot account for, when there has been no moral defection. The light of eternity has been suffered to pass off from the objects of faith and the acts of devotion.

If you are not fully aware of this, or did not observe how much a sense of eternity blended with all your first and strongest impressions of divine things, the consideration of it will amply repay you for both the time and thought it calls for.

Now, at whatever point of truth your serious impressions began, the *force* of that point was derived from eternity. Even if your heart was first moved and melted by the *love of Christ*, this is the fact of the case. You, indeed, thought of nothing, at the moment, but the glories, grace, and sacrifice of the Lamb of God. All your wonder and gratitude were concentrated upon his person and work. He was "All and All, and altogether lovely," in the views which then captivated and conquered your heart. And, had any one said to you, at that sacred moment, that you were thinking of eternity, you would have replied, "I think, I can think, of nothing but the amazing and melting love of my Saviour; and of my own guilt and folly, in not thinking of it sooner."

There was, however, much reference to eternity in all this process and pressure of thought and feeling. You, indeed, were not conscious of it; because, like sun-light on flowers, the light of eternity does not divide our attention between itself and the objects it shines on. It was, however, there; blended with, and beautifying, every view of the Saviour and salvation. Accordingly, had you analyzed your own thoughts at the time, or afterwards, you would have found that they had not only glanced alternately at the past and future eternity of the love of Christ; but, also, that its eternity was the very *crown* of its worth and glory. For, had He not loved for eternity, and redeemed for eternity, you could not have thought nor felt as you did. Had any doubt of eternity itself, or of the eternal duration of his love, mingled with your meditations, they would not have been transporting nor transforming in their influence.

There was, however, more than an undoubting recognition of eternity, in your adoring views of the Saviour. They were based upon, and blended with, a settled and solemn persuasion of the immortality of your soul. Your spirit, although unconscious of its own transitions between eternity and the cross, was yet, and all the while, glancing from the one to the other, and linking both together. Its movements were too numerous and rapid to be felt as transitions of thought or feeling, at the moment; but, now that you begin to analyze them, you perceive that you were employing the glories of the cross to soften eternity, and the glories of eternity to enshrine the cross. Thus all your most realizing and influential views of the Lamb slain, were full of immortality.

Eternity was all around the cross, as the flood around the ark ; and though your eye, in its intended and intense gaze, was fixed, like the dove's, on the refuge ; like her's, also, it darted sidelong and swift and perpetual glances on the surrounding waters.

Now, as this was the real character of your first and finest views of the Saviour and salvation, and as they derived so much of their power and glory from their connection with eternity, it is not wonderful that both their power and their glory should decay, whenever you lose sight of eternity, or cease to look at the cross in the light of it.

In like manner, if your personal piety began in a deep sense of the value of your *soul*, that solemn conviction derived its chief solemnity from eternity. It was more than based on, or blended with, the consciousness of immortality : it was "full" of immortality. It would have been powerless, yea, been nothing, but for eternity. For, whatever you thought or felt, in regard to any or all the powers of the mind, it was the fact of their being eternal powers, that arrested and riveted your attention. It was memory, as remembering for ever ; it was imagination, as creative for ever ; it was reason, as reasoning for ever ; it was conscience, as judging for ever; that awed and amazed you. Eternal consciousness! eternal thought! eternal feeling! was the absorbing consideration. It was not mental power, as mental; nor moral sense, as moral; but the eternity of mind and conscience, that impressed you. It was not the degree in which the soul was capable of enjoying or suffering; but the "everlasting" *duration* of future joy or wo, that determined you to care for your soul. Accordingly, had its faculties been both fewer and feebler, and even incapable of any improvement, here or hereafter, their eternity would have stamped and sustained them as infinitely valuable, in your estimation. And, as they must advance for ever, as well as endure for ever, you certainly did not overrate their value, when you resolved not to lose your soul.

Now, if these solemn views of the immortality of your spirit have been allowed to pass away, or to languish into cold and heartless forms of thought, it is not surprising that you should kneel at the mercy-seat without enjoyment, and at the cross without feeling. For, how can the soul, when it has become almost insensible to its own immortal nature, and immense value, and amazing faculties, feel alive in prayer or meditation? How can the throne of grace be attractive, or the cross dear, "as in the days of old," when you no longer come to them under a deep or distinct consciousness of your immortality?

The want, or the weakness, of this, is just as incompatible with a devotional spirit, as the want or weakness of humility, penitence, or faith. Now, you are fully aware, that a self-righteous, or a self-sufficient spirit, does not, and cannot, find communion with God, nor comfort from the promises. You know well, that if you forget your guilt or weakness, you are neither successful nor urgent in prayer. Accordingly, you find it necessary, and make it convenient, to keep up a habitual sense of your sinfulness and unworthiness, that thus you may be humble before God, whenever you appear before Him in the sanctuary or the closet. All this is as it should be. The habitual consciousness of immortality is, however, as necessary as humility. Indeed, humility will not be very deep, when the sense of immortality is dim. The latter is not, indeed, like the former, one of the "graces" of the Spirit; but it is the element in which they were all born, and out of which none of them thrive well. We are not repenting well, when we are not repenting for eternity; nor believing well, when we are not believing for eternity;

nor praying well, when we are not praying with an express reference to eternity.

It is, therefore, of supreme importance to acquire and keep up a vivid sense of immortality, if you would keep up the power of your principles, and the exercise of your graces. It is as an immortal spirit, that your soul will be most reverential in the presence of "the Father of spirits;" and most humble in the presence of "the Father of mercies;" and most believing in the presence of "the Father of lights." It is as an immortal spirit, it will best worship the Eternal Spirit "in spirit and truth."

If, again, your personal piety began in deep and solemn convictions of the *evil of sin*, they, too, derived both their depth and solemnity from the fact, that the punishment of sin is eternal. This is true, even if your convictions arose chiefly from the manifestation of the evil of sin, which is given by the cross of Christ. Now, nowhere else does sin appear so "exceeding sinful," as in the agony and ignominy of the Saviour. That his blood was required in order to atone for it, throws every other proof of its evil into the shade; and is the only proof that *silences* all the questions and equivocations of unbelief. Abstract reasonings about sin being an infinite evil, because committed against an infinite God; and because its tendency is to dethrone God; and because its nature is to go on from bad to worse for ever and ever, do not, whatever be the cause of their failure, bring home an *abiding* conviction of the evil of sin. However true the logic, or legitimate the conclusions, of such reasonings may be, sophistry can wind its way through, or wing its way over them all, if they are not hung upon the cross of Christ. Accordingly, those who see nothing in the cross but a martyr's altar, see nothing in sin but a temporary evil, pardonable apart from all atonement. None of their views of God or man alarm them at sin ; except when it is so gross as to be disgraceful, or so horrid as to be shocking.

But even where Calvary produces a conviction of sin, which Sinai could not do; and the gospel a fear of sin, which the law cannot implant, both derive their point and power from eternity. And in this way,—the punishment of sin being eternal in its duration, when it is inflicted upon sinners, what must have been the amount and intensity of the Saviour's sufferings, when his soul was made " an offering for sin ? " " Wrath to the uttermost " is not inflicted by God, for the sake of trying what its " uttermost" is. Neither the degree nor the duration of it in hell, is, or can be, any pleasure to Him. He has actually sworn by his life, that he has " no pleasure " in the death of a sinner. Its very uttermost is, therefore, the very *least* that, in justice to his own character and government, he can inflict. And, as that least is eternal, there must have been in the Saviour's " cup," a bitterness, unspeakable and inconceivable to men or angels. If, however, this view of the evil of sin belong to that class of proofs, which do not implant abiding convictions, because they do not impale themselves beyond all controversy, still, it is from eternity, in some form, that the death of Christ derives its unspeakable power of " convincing of sin." We, indeed, may not see nor feel this, whilst beholding the Lamb of God taking away the sin of the world. The glory veiled, and the vials broken, and the agonies endured, on that solemn occasion, seem more than enough, without a reference to eternity, to account for all our deepest convictions of the evil of sin. The darkness and tempest around the cross, whilst they cover and convulse the heavens and the earth, seem to render all reference to the eternal " blackness of darkness " unnecessary. But even on Calvary, and at the very crisis of the atoning sacrifice, eternity is present to the mind, however much it may be absorbed with the sufferings of Christ. For, were a doubt of the eternal punishment of sin to flash across the mind, at that moment; or were the wrath he redeemed from not eternal; both the dread and the hatred of sin, which the cross inspires, would not be what they are in the heart of believers. But we are, however unconsciously and unintentionally, glancing from time to time at the eternity of the wrath which He is delivering from. There is mingled with all our emotions of grief and gratitude, a real, though secret, reference to the eternity of misery, which, but for his atonement, would have been our inevitable portion; and to the eternity of happiness which, by faith in his atonement, may be our inheritance.

This is only saying in other words, that we are not insensible to the *design* of the atonement, whilst most affected by its solemnities. Indeed, the very reason why our thoughts and feelings are so concentrated on the cross, and so absorbed by the wonders of redemption, is because the redemption of the cross is eternal. For, were it not so, neither its attraction nor its influence could be so powerful. It being, therefore, self-evident that eternity set the confirming seal upon those convictions of the evil and danger of sin, which shut us up to Christ for pardon, and to the Spirit for sanctification, it is certain that sin, if shifted out of this light, will not be so dreaded as to endear the cross, nor so hated as to honor the Holy Spirit. For as we should not have fled to the Saviour or to the Sanctifier, had we not seen the flaming sword of the law in the hand of eternity, neither shall we cleave to them steadfastly, if we cease to view sin in this connection. Nor is this all: there is no small danger of even tampering with sin, if it be not looked at in this light. All backsliding of heart and life is brought on by losing sight of eternity. No one forsakes " the fountain of living waters,' whilst its waters sparkle with the light of eternity. No one drinks from polluted streams, until he has shaded them from that light.

If, again, your personal piety began in impressive and exalted views of the *divine character and government*, it was eternity that invested them with power and glory. Whatever lovely view of God first affected and won your heart, the perfection of its beauty was in the fact, that " this God is our God, for ever and ever." Whatever solemn view of God awed your spirit, its weight lay in the consideration, that "from everlasting," such had been his majesty, and "to everlasting," such it would be. Whatever attraction or terror brought you under the shadow of his wings, the full sense of safety came from this, "the eternal God is thy refuge." And whenever you have felt through all your soul, that his "loving kindness is better than life," it was the eternity of it that eclipsed the charms of life, and softened the aspect of death.

The fact is, that, in all our *first* intentional and deliberate contemplations of God, and approaches to God, we were thinking and acting with an express reference to eternity: for, at first, they had nothing else to terminate upon. Now, that we have a name, or a place, or both, to maintain in the church and the world, our prayers and meditations often terminate on them. Our immediate solicitude often goes no farther than to be kept from forfeiting or disgracing our profession; whereas, before we made a public profession of religion, it went all the length of eternal safety at once. Now, however, we usually advance to this final point, step by step. It is, of course, still our goal: but, at first, it was both our goal and our starting-place. We began and ended our devotional exercises, with an express regard to our future state. We had not then given to the world or the church, solemn pledges of faith or repentance. We had not committed ourselves, publicly, to any creed, service, or connection. All our piety was then personal; and irresponsible to man. It implicated the character of no church, nor the tendency of any system. All its actings had their source and centre in our individual salvation. But now, they have other bearings and motives; and these, although not different from the former, are yet distinct enough to divide our attention between time and eternity. Accordingly, many of our prayers, and more of our thoughts, terminate upon present consistency, rather than upon future safety; upon living well, rather than upon dying well.

This, of course, is not to be regretted. Our daily prayers and meditations ought to bear, with point and power, on the duties and trials of the day. We cannot die happy, if we do not live to some good purpose. It is, however, equally true, that the concentration of all our solicitude upon a godly life, is not the best way of maintaining personal godliness. More than effort is necessary, in order to follow holiness well. Motives must be freely admitted, if rules and laws are to be cheerfully or impartially obeyed. In a word; our time will not be well spent, if our eternity be seldom realized. Whilst, therefore, it would be highly improper to lessen our attention to the practical duties of life or godliness, it is also highly imprudent to allow even them to divert our attention from eternity. But for its solemn influence, we had never believed nor obeyed the gospel from the heart; and, therefore, that influence must be cherished, if we would continue to believe or obey. Having begun as immortal, we must not go on as mortal. Having set out as the children of eternity, we must not subside into mere children of time. That would be another form of the Galatian error. Gal. iii. 3.

No. VI.

FAITH, BELIEVING UNTO ETERNAL LIFE.

Well might the believing of the primitive Christians be called, "precious faith," and "most holy faith:" for its influence upon their *spirits* was equally soothing and cheering; and upon their *character*, equally ennobling and sanctifying. No man can think lightly of their joy or peace in believing. Their joy was "unspeakable and full of glory;" and their peace surpassed "all understanding." Every one whose heart has ever ached, whose conscience has ever smarted, whose spirits have ever been low, can and must envy such joy and peace. Even our modern Balaams, who are absorbed in the love of the world, must acknowledge that this is a joy which the world cannot give, and a peace which they do not find; for even they have intervals of depression and pain which quite qualify them, at the time, to comprehend how the first Christians were happier in poverty, than they are with wealth. And, if worldlings can judge thus, from mere "vexation of spirit," no wonder if we who have had, in addition to our share of that vexation, spiritual discoveries of our guilt and danger, should envy the spiritual happiness of the primitive believers. We can appreciate their joy as saints, because we have experienced something of their sorrows and fears as sinners. Our souls have been in their soul's place, when "the iron entered" into them; and, therefore, we naturally wish our souls to be also in their place, when all their wounds were healed, and all their fears dispelled. We have joined them in the solemn question, "What shall I do to be saved?" and, therefore, we wish to join them in the triumphant song, "Unto him who loved us, and washed us from our sins in his own blood." We have had fellowship of spirit with them in the piercing cry, "Lord, save, I perish;" and we desire communion with them in the grateful acknowledgment, "He hath saved us, and called us with an holy calling." We have been partakers of their fears of the wrath to come; and, therefore, we long to be partakers of their good and lively hope of the glory to be revealed.

Not—that we are utter strangers to all peace or joy in believing. It is because we have tasted something of both, that we are so intent on "drinking abundantly" of the cup of salvation. The difference between our spiritual happiness, and that of the first believers, is not one of *kind*, but of degree. They seem to have had an *abiding* spirit of adoption; an abiding sense of pardon and acceptance; an abiding witness of the Holy Spirit; an abiding confidence in the wisdom of Providence and the sufficiency of grace. I mean, abiding, as compared with the extreme changeableness of modern joy and peace. Their happiness was not absolutely unchangeable, nor uniform; but their alterations of hope and fear—of light and darkness—of assurance and doubt, were neither so great nor any thing like so frequent as our changes. This is so true and striking, that we have often questioned the reality of our own faith, on the single ground of its failing to produce such joy and peace as they experienced. Indeed, we are sometimes tempted to suspect, that much of their comfort must have sprung from the *miraculous* gifts of the Spirit, as well as from his gracious influences; and that, thus, it is impossible to acquire, now, so much enjoyment. This, however, even if true to a far greater extent than can be proved or suspected, was counterbalanced by the peculiar and manifold trials of the primitive Christians. Any miraculous gifts which the generality had, were not more than a counterpoise to their fiery trials, from which we are exempt. Our dispensation of Providence is a better boon, and more adapted to promote spiritual enjoyment, than their dispensation of the Spirit—so far it was miraculous. Accordingly, neither their joy nor peace is ever explained, by a reference to their *gifts*, but always ascribed to the abundance of grace. As the Saviour taught the apostles and evangelists to rejoice, "because their names were written in heaven," so they taught their converts to find their comfort in the everlasting gospel itself, and not in evanescent endowments. We must not look at circumstances, therefore, for the secret of that "strong consolation" which was so common in the apostolic churches. Nothing that was supernatural in their lot, exceeded what was trying to flesh and blood in it. As on the globe, the greatest seas are hung opposite the greatest mountains, to balance them, so floods of affliction were not more than counterpoised by miracles.

What, then, was the real *secret* of that copious, calm, and holy enjoyment, which the first believers so habitually possessed? They had no foundation of hope, that we have not: no warrant or welcome to build on the Rock of Ages, that we have not: no promises nor prospects, that we have not. Jesus Christ is the same in our "day," as He was in their "yesterday." The Tree of Life bends its loaded and luxuriant branches, as fully down to our hands, as it did to their hands. Why is it, then, that whilst we see those who came first around that tree, healed by its leaves, and cheered by its fruit, many of us are afraid to taste, and more of us but half healed and half refreshed? Now, the fact is, they "eat" for the express and immediate purpose that they might "Live for ever." Their faith was, from the beginning to the end, a direct "looking for the mercy of our Lord Jesus Christ unto eternal life."

This fact, thus stated, may not strike you at first sight. There is, however, more in it than meets the eye at once. *Immediate* and *express* believing for eternal life, is not so common nor so habitual as it seems. All real faith has, of course, eternal life as its grand and final object; and, in this respect, we, as much as the first believers, have, as the end of our faith, "the salvation" of our souls, "with eternal joy." But, if we make this a *remote* object; and if they made it their immediate object; there will, there must, be a difference between our faith and theirs, as to *degree*, which cannot fail to produce a corresponding difference of comfort. Now, what is the sober fact, in regard to the ordinary and every-day exercise of our faith in Christ? The truth is, it neither embraces nor aims at much beyond *safety for the day;* and the consequence is, that it gathers but little strength from such exercise. On days of peculiar trial or temptation, it is put upon the stretch, and compelled to draw largely upon the provisions of the everlasting covenant. In like manner, on days of peculiar refreshing in the sanctuary, it is charmed into lively exercise and lofty aspiration. But, in general, these extraordinary actings of faith are called forth by extraordinary circumstances; and, accordingly, whilst we are not much tried or tempted, nor powerfully stirred up by spirit-stirring appeals, we put forth no more faith than just what will keep us from going back in religion; and, alas, not always so much! Now, such tame and restricted believing cannot lead to much or strong consolation. It is not *conversant* with the sources of spiritual comfort. Paul, with all his charity, would not say to us, whilst our faith was thus idle, " Now the God of hope fill you with joy and peace in believing." *Such* believing would incur his censure, or throw him upon his knees to pray for an increase of our faith.

We must, however, go still deeper into the ordinary state of our minds, before we can see clearly the grand cause of the difference between the degree of our own comfort, and that of the first believers. Now our tendency is, to defer believing for eternity, until we come to the *verge* of eternity. We do not like to bring the matter of final safety to a full issue every day; nor to go far into it any day, whilst we feel no pressing occasion. Like those who shrink from making their last WILL, lest such a distinct recognition of their mortality should shorten their life, we are inclined to leave the question of our personal safety unsettled, whilst we are in health. We have no objection to such a state of mind, from day to day, as would furnish all the materials for dying well, if a sudden summons should come. We are even willing to be, to a considerable extent, "as men waiting for the coming of their Lord." Not, however, alas! because we long or wish for his coming; we do not desire it, until we have no other prospect; but we do feel the necessity of not forgetting it, nor preparation for it, altogether. We dread the bare idea of being found "asleep," or with "lamps gone out," when our Lord cometh. We wish to have our lamps so far filled and trimmed, that they shall burst into a steady flame, the moment we are called to meet the Bridegroom. This is, however, almost all that we can say, with perfect truth, concerning the habitual tone of our piety. We leave much to be done and settled on our death-bed. We content ourselves with doing pretty well from day to day; and postpone to our last days, the full settlement of our personal interest in Christ. So much uncertainty do we allow to hang over this question, that we actually promise to crowd the close of life with mightier and more pointed acts of faith on the Son of God, than any that we put forth now. And we feel that it will be *necessary* to do so then, if we would be either triumphant or tranquil in death. Hence

ETERNAL LIFE.

the intense solicitude we occasionally pour into that hymn,

> "O for an overcoming faith,
> To cheer my dying hours!"

Now all this shows how little immediate and express reference our daily faith has to eternal life. It terminates more on present comfort than on future safety; on momentary ease, than on everlasting glory. And then—it is so easy to believe for all the daily mercy and grace which we *feel* in need of, whilst there is nothing very trying in our lot, that our faith is not able to meet emergencies, when they come unexpectedly upon us. In fact, we suspect that it is little better than *unbelief*, when we feel how it fails, whenever we are compelled to look death steadfastly in the face. I pray you to mark this usual effect of the prospect of death, on our ordinary faith. When any thing like a mortal qualm quivers around the heart; or any disorder assumes a fatal aspect; or any stroke of death falls so near us as to stun us, or as to startle us into a keen sense of personal and pressing danger, we naturally betake ourselves to the exercise of believing prayer. Knowing that to be our only resource, we flee to it at once. But, lo! all is hurry, and flutter, and confusion, in our spirit. We seem to have no faith! Like Hezekiah, we turn our face to the wall, and weep bitterly; we are so shocked to find that we had contented ourselves with a kind of faith which seldom, or but slightly, faced the dread solemnities of death and eternity; or with a degree of faith, which had always shrunk from them, and now sunk under them.

These are awful moments, and humiliating discoveries! How we upbraid ourselves during their pressure, for the indecision, the folly, the infatuation, of a process of believing, which did not go all the length of looking daily for mercy, "unto eternal life." How we resolve that, if spared, we will make sure work for eternity; and enter upon a new life of faith on the Son of God, which shall *deserve* the name of faith. Accordingly, we did, for a time, after being thus startled and humbled, set ourselves in good earnest, to believe unto the saving of our souls, with an everlasting salvation. We returned to the point and spirit of our first applications to the Saviour. We knelt at the mercy-seat, laying hold of the cross with one hand, and of eternal life with the other hand. We thus kept in view the final end of faith, as well as its immediate objects; and honestly told ourselves, that any thing less than meeting the whole question of final safety, must render the next approach of death as overwhelming as the former.

We remember all this well. It is, therefore, humiliating to confess, that, notwithstanding this solemn lesson, and after acting on it for some time, we have again and again relapsed into our old habit of resting in *half* measures; and of living, praying, and believing, *for the day*, and not for eternity. We continue, indeed, "looking for the mercy of our Lord Jesus Christ," every day; but not, every day, looking for it, "unto eternal life."

By this time you are willing to go into the question, how came the primitive Christians to acquire such a realizing and habitual sense of the glory and solemnity of eternal life? How did they manage to keep on believing *up* to the "*end*" of faith? The real answer to this question cannot be short, and satisfactory too. It is necessary, in order to understand their case, to have the whole of it before us, both in substance and detail.

Observe, then, how their faith was solicited and enforced, in the first instance. Now, it was not claimed, at the outset, by temporal nor by temporary considerations. The first appeals they heard, on behalf of faith in Christ, were not founded on the reasonableness of faith; nor on its holy influence; nor on the mere criminality of unbelief; but on the eternal advantages of believing in Christ. Everlasting happiness was the *first* thing proposed to them by the gospel. It said nothing to them about the beauty or the necessity of holiness, until it had made to them a full disclosure, and a free offer, of that glorious heaven, which deserves all the holiness it demands;—nothing to them about the duty or the privilege of prayer, until it had presented to them the prospect of that eternal communion with God and the Lamb, of which prayer is the pledge and the prelude;—nothing to them about joining the church, or celebrating her sacraments, until it had tried upon their souls all the attractions of the church of the first-born, and of the marriage-supper of the Lamb, in heaven. Thus eternal life was the grand thing which they began to believe on Christ for. Their faith did not, indeed, stop there: nor was it allowed to overlook any of the practical designs of the gospel. It was not, however, made, in the first instance, to travel through them, step by step, until it reached the hope of glory, as the *result* of obedience;

but it was lifted to that immortal hope at once, and then led into all the paths of virtue and holiness. Thus an almost personified eternity, in all its grandeur, placed before them the high claims of the Saviour on their confidence and subjection. Their faith was asked and won, amidst vivid visions of the pealing harps, the sparkling crowns, and the eternal mansions, of the general assembly in heaven. Nor was this all. That "opened" heaven came before them, confronted with an equally opened hell. They had, therefore, in believing, to look all that glory, and all that wrath, full in the face; and to believe *up* to the point of deliverance from that wrath, and of a title to that glory.

Now, need I say that, in order to the exercise of such faith, they must have looked closer and oftener at " the mercy of our Lord Jesus Christ," than if they had only been believing in order to be fit for baptism and the sacrament; or for the purpose of becoming better, and being in the right way ? You see, at a glance, that their views of his mercy must have been as vast and vivid as their views of heaven and hell; and their faith in his mercy as strong as their faith in eternal things. Slight notions of the person or work of Christ, and doubtful faith in Him, would not have lifted them over the fear of perishing, nor up to the hope of salvation. And, as they found enough in the Lamb slain to meet all the wants and perils of their case, no wonder if they continued looking for his mercy unto eternal life. The *needle* of their faith was so magnetized by eternity at first, that it turned to that pole for ever after.

Now, did our believing begin thus? Had it such a full and distinct reference to " eternal redemption?" Perhaps not exactly. It had, however, a pointed reference to escape from the wrath to come, at first; and, if it has a less pointed one now, that is one reason why our comfort is less than that of the primitive believers. They did not satisfy themselves with believing that their escape was possible; nor with believing that it was not improbable; nor with believing that they were as likely to escape as others. They did not hush up nor hurry over the great question in this sluggish and superficial way. They seem to have both avoided and disdained that *half-way* faith, which places itself just so near the Refuge, that it can, as it imagines, flee into it on a moment's warning. Indeed, they seem to have had no idea of that paltry policy in religion, which just abstains from going altogether *out of sight* of the Cross, or *out of reach* of the

Refuge : but which abstains equally from coming under their shadow or their authority. This was not the religion of the first Christians. Nothing stifled or stilled their cry, " What shall we do to be saved," but a faith which could say, " We believe that through the grace of our Lord Jesus, we shall be saved." Even good signs did not satisfy them. We never hear any of them banishing or balancing their sense of danger, by an appeal to the *convictions* they felt under one sermon ; or to the *tears* they shed under another ; or to the *vows* they made at the sacrament; or to the *prayers* they poured out in the day of trouble. They did not, of course, think lightly of these things, nor exclude them from the catalogue of experimental exercises : but neither did they rest in them as grounds of safety, nor allow them to keep the soul from making a full and final committal of itself into the hands of Christ. Indeed, they could not compromise their safety in this way; because they did not, or durst not, shut their eyes on either the eternal heaven which had captivated them, nor on the eternal hell which had alarmed them.

Now, if we feel that there has been, in our own case, a less impression of, or a less reference to, heaven and hell; and, that in consequence of this estrangement of our thoughts from eternity, we have rather gone on looking for mercy, "unto" a *long* life, or an *easy* life, or even a *good* life, than "unto eternal life;" it is necessary, and it is high time, to resume our first views of the great salvation, and even to brighten them by profounder meditation.

Another circumstance which gave point and power to the faith of the first Christians was, that they were the *first*. I do not mean by this, the sublimity nor the responsibility of the distinction. They could hardly be aware of either, for some time. What I mean is, that they were not influenced in their believing, by the *memory* of their parents and other departed friends; and, thus, were in no danger of mistaking an hereditary creed, for personal faith; or veneration of a parent's piety, for love to his God and Saviour. They had no *family* links between their hearts and heaven, when they began to believe unto eternal life. No last injunction of a dying father or mother induced them to flee from the wrath to come. None of the Gentiles, at least, had upon their soul a solemn charge from any departing spirit, to prepare to meet it on the right of the Judge; but each convert had to act on the force of his own convictions, and of his own faith in the gospel.

Now, this, although no enviable position, was not unfavorable to decision of character. The very pain of these circumstances promoted sincerity and promptitude. Every Gentile convert had to act for himself, and on his own resources, in forming those views of faith and practice, which form the character for heaven. Whatever, therefore, he lacked of relative motive, he was not diverted from personal decision, by family hopes or habits.

We cannot, of course, regret, but must rejoice, that heaven comes before us not desolate of ancestral spirits. It is no small part of our happiness to believe, that some of those, who were nearest and dearest to us on earth, are now before the throne; and even there continue to love us, and to long for us to join them. These are golden links between our hearts and heaven! and might be expected, as they are well calculated, to draw our thoughts and affections very often and very far heavenward. And they have this sweet influence, whenever we allow them to exert it. It is, however, necessary to take care lest this ardent love to those who are " for ever with the Lord," be mistaken for love to the Lord himself. For, although we cannot love them too ardently, we are in danger of loving him too coldly; and of looking more at heaven in the softened form of meeting *them*, than in the solemn form of meeting God. It was in the latter form chiefly, that the first Christians looked at eternity; and, therefore, their piety was an habitual preparation to meet God. And, surely, ours ought not, need not, to be different, seeing we expect to meet so many endeared spirits at the same time with him! For, so far as this fond hope softens the solemn interview which we anticipate, so far it ought to increase and quicken our anticipations of it.

Another circumstance which gave great point and conclusiveness to the faith of the first believers, was, the peril of life at which they became Christians. An open and avowed " looking for the mercy of the Lord Jesus Christ, unto eternal life," was, in fact, the risking of *temporal* life, as well as of property, and freedom, and reputation. It required, therefore, an habitual looking at the things which are unseen and eternal, in order to balance at all the loss of the things which are seen and temporal. Nothing less than such a familiarity with their " enduring substance in heaven," could have reconciled or enabled them to peril life and substance on earth, as they did.

Their heavenly-mindedness was not, however, the virtue of *necessity*, on their part. They did not take up with heaven, because of the peculiar uncertainty of life and property at the time ; but, for the sake of eternal life, they voluntarily and deliberately hazarded every thing. Their privations were the effects, not the cause, of their choice. Nor did they repent of that choice, when its effects proved fatal. In vain, therefore, do we attempt to excuse, by the tendency of easier circumstances, our inferior heavenly-mindedness. We are not, indeed, thrown so directly and constantly on eternity for comfort, as they were. We have more " vineyards in the wilderness " than they had. The lines are fallen to us in pleasant places, and we have a goodly heritage, compared with their lot. But, do we, dare we, turn this into a reason, or an excuse, for thinking but seldom and slightly of the glory to be revealed ? A heart thoroughly and habitually "right with God," would find in this change for the better, nothing but reasons and motives for a higher degree of heavenly-mindedness;

because we thus possess more time, and convenience, and composure, for devotional habits.

Besides, there is even in the ordinary uncertainty of life, what ought to be quite enough to turn the eye upon eternity *every* day. How often we are shocked or surprised by sudden deaths, in the circle of our own acquaintance? How often we see that no age, however promising, and no office, however important, is any absolute security against sudden death? And now that Pestilence is in the country, how loud is the call, " Be ye also ready?" That virulent disease leaves neither time nor power for clearing up doubtful conversions, or for healing backslidings. Its victims must go into eternity in the *dark*, if it find them unprepared or ill prepared. It gives no space for repentance, and no intervals for prayer. As the tree stands it must fall, and as it falls it must lie, beneath the stroke of this axe! Those only are prepared for this death, who are believing " unto eternal life."

No. VII.

ETERNITY REALIZED IN THE SANCTUARY.

If Jacob could regard his anointed pillar on Bethel, as "none other than the house of God," and, therefore, as "the gate of heaven," we may well and easily recognise in the Christian sanctuary, the gate of heaven; for its oracles and ordinances reveal far more of heaven than the vision of the mystic ladder did, and are far more calculated to make us meet for the inheritance of the saints in light. We, indeed, see no angels ascending or descending in the house of God; but we have, in its lively oracles and expressive ordinances, what is more instructive than any vision of *silent* angels could be; for Jacob's angels were all silent on Bethel. God, indeed, spake to him there; but, how little, compared with our ample volume of revelation.

It is quite needless to contrast farther our "gate of heaven," with that on Bethel: it is, however, very necessary to compare our own views and feelings towards the sanctuary, with those of Jacob; for, if he loved and revered Bethel, as a pledge and prelude of the heavenly temple, it surely becomes us to imitate him in our Zion. It is more like heaven, and more linked to it, than any anointed pillar on a bleak mountain could be, however consecrated. When the ministers of the sanctuary affirm this fact, and, on the ground of it, enforce regular and reverential attendance on public worship, they as much proclaim what their own character and preaching ought to be, as what our character and feelings ought to be. An unholy minister never exposes himself more to contempt, than when he stands forward to assert a connection between *his* sanctuary and heaven; and thus to enforce its claims on our regard. We both dispute and despise the claim, so far as he is concerned.

It is a very different dilemma, but still a real dilemma, when a minister, although not unholy, has neither talents nor learning to justify at all the demands upon our attention, which he puts forward in the name of the sanctuary and the Sabbath. Their claims and his are certainly not identical. We cannot acquire knowledge from an ignorant man, nor wisdom from a weak man, however good his character or his intentions may be. Indeed, the weightier the claims of the house and day of God are, the lighter are those of men,

"Who cannot teach, and will not learn;"

and yet, unfortunately, such men are most forward to mix themselves up with the divine authority of religious ordinances.

Eminently holy ministers, of inferior acquirements, never fall into this mistake, nor place themselves in this awkward dilemma. Their superior holiness renders it impossible for them to talk or think of what is owing to their office in the church. Accordingly, their only wonder is, and it is sincere, that their ministry is attended at all. Worthy men! In the godly simplicity of their hearts, they forget that there is a charm in their holy and heavenly unction, which no judicious Christian would exchange for mere eloquence or learning. Such shepherds will never be without a flock, whilst there are sheep or lambs in the fold of God, who prefer refreshment to amusement, and food to excitement. The success of men, who are lost in their message, is neither marvellous nor mysterious. Humanly speaking, it may be " a wonder unto many;" but, *divinely* speaking, it is only what might be expected.

But, whatever be the talents, the acquirements, or the piety of a minister, he places himself in a very delicate position, whenever he commends or enforces the claims of the house of God, as "the gate of heaven." We ought, then, to hear him with great candor, and even to sympathise with him; for the question, "Is my preaching in character, is my spirit in harmony, with these high claims?" is pressing heavily on his heart. The bare consideration, that neither his ministerial character nor spirit is in *contrast* to the heavenliness of the sanctuary, is not enough, when *this* is his theme, to maintain his usual composure! He feels through all his soul, that *words* will not prove to us, that the house of God is the gate of heaven. He is penetrated with the conviction, that assertions, however solemn, and arguments, however strong, will and must fail to imbue us with the spirit of Jacob, unless a double portion of that heavenly spirit rest upon himself. He even feels sure, that the more Zion is complimented in words, the less she will be venerated, unless his own unction illustrate her claims. Such a man, therefore, deserves both our candor and gratitude, whenever he tries to dignify or endear the sanctuary, by proving that

"The Holy to the HOLIEST leads."

It is, then, desirable and necessary, that our ministers should regard the house of God as the gate of heaven ; and both preach and pray under a realizing sense of this sublime fact. Without the cultivation of this spirit and habit on their part, there will be a lack of spirituality on our part. It should not, however, depend chiefly on the minister, whether the ordinances and fellowship of Zion shall, or shall not, be to us, the foretastes of heaven. We have free access to all the sources, both of information and influence, which warrant or enable him to connect the church on earth with the church in heaven. Let us, therefore, familiarize ourselves, devotionally, with those scriptural views of the sanctuary, which are most heavenly; that thus we may feel its claims to love and veneration, even when he fails to plead them in demonstration of the Spirit ; and that we may enjoy its ordinances when he succeeds in throwing the light of eternity upon them.

Now, it would be strange, indeed, if the

house of God were not represented in the Scriptures, as the gate of heaven. It must be so,—if the character of God be the same in heaven as it is on earth. It must be so,— if the first principles and final end of his worship be the same in both worlds. This is self-evident. God would not teach us on earth, what we should have to unlearn in heaven. He would not train us here, on principles which had no place there. No; we are now learning the lessons, and acquiring the character, which eternity will perfect and perpetuate. The paternal and covenant character of God in Christ, has no change to undergo, when we exchange worlds. It will be more clearly seen, and more fully enjoyed, as to degrees of light and joy, but not as to kind. God, as he is now known in Zion, will be " our God for ever and ever."

Were there nothing to endear the sanctuary to us but this one fact, we might well regard it as the gate of heaven. No work nor wonder of nature presents the divine character in that light, in which it is seen and enjoyed in the upper sanctuary. Paternal views of God may be transferred from his house to his creation; but no scene of creation is a gate of heaven. The loveliest is too cold, and the sublimest too dark, to shadow forth "our Father," as he is "in heaven." This, however, the oracles and ordinances of Zion do effectually. They present God to us, in the very relation in which he stands, and will sustain for ever, towards all the redeemed spirits before his throne.

How this fact ought to dignify and endear Zion in our estimation! Its courts are more than "holy ground;" they are *heavenly* too. David understood the matter thus, when he said, "One thing have I desired of the Lord, and that will I seek after, that I may dwell in the house of the Lord all the days of my life, to behold the beauty of the Lord." He knew that His beauty there, was the same in substance as in the heaven of heavens; and, therefore, he gave a decided preference to that place where God appears likest to what He is and ever will be, on the throne. Let this be present to our minds, whenever we appear before God in Zion. Let us say to ourselves as we go to his house,—I am about to contemplate God, and to commune with Him, in the very character which he will sustain through eternity. There is that in his paternal love and glory, which will for ever secure my love, and delight my soul, when all my powers are perfect and immortal. I shall never, never tire of viewing him as my father; and never, never fail to find joy unspeakable from this near and dear relationship. It will gratify and satisfy me to all eternity. Surely, then, I may well love the place where he most displays his paternal character; and well fill up the time with a theme that will fill eternity.

We may not, indeed, always enter into the spirit of this consideration, when we enter the sanctuary; but, by attempting to do so always, we shall learn a valuable lesson even when we fail. Let us, therefore, say to ourselves, when we leave the house of God without delight in his character,—An eternity of this estrangement of heart from God, would be intolerable! An eternity of dark and harsh views of God would be horrible! Why should I ever entertain such views? The house of God is the gate of heaven; and, therefore, I am warranted to cherish such views of his character now, as will, when perfect, cheer me for ever. Let me not, then, indulge ideas of God, which I would not carry into heaven. Let me not think of Him now, as I shall never think of Him

"Whilst immortality endures."

The connection of the house of God with

the SAVIOUR, also, renders it emphatically the gate of heaven. The grand reason why nature presents no gates of heaven, is, that it gives no intimations of a Saviour. There is nothing in all the range of its most radiant glories which suggests one idea of heaven; except so far as revelation has employed them as emblems of it. Apart from that, they throw no light upon the invisible world. But the sanctuary is so founded upon Christ, and so full of express references to him, that it is very like all that we know of heaven, both as a state, and as a place. The determination of ministers to know nothing amongst us, save Jesus Christ, and him crucified, is akin to the constancy with which saints and angels sing, " Worthy is the Lamb that was slain." The adoring humility and gratitude with which believers ascribe all their salvation to Him, are not unlike the emotions which lead all the spirits of the just to cast their crowns at his feet. The church on earth, at the sacramental supper, is not altogether unlike the church in heaven, at the marriage supper of the Lamb. " The new song " of both churches is the same. And when the whole assembly mingle their hearts and voices in the grand Hallelujah chorus of that song, there is nothing on earth so like unto heaven. There are, indeed, many and sad dissimilarities; and it would be unwise to forget them. But still, after making all the deductions which truth requires, there remains more of the aspect and spirit of heaven in Zion, than can be found in any other assembly. There is, alas, too little of the image of Christ, and less of his spirit, in his churches; but, nowhere else is there so much of either. It is, therefore, both unwise and improper to allow the imperfections, or even the spots, of the church on earth, to hide from us her relationship and resemblance to heaven. He is only "wise in his own conceit," who stands aloof from her fellowship, under the pretence that no church is pure enough for his taste. Such wilful "aliens from the commonwealth of Israel," are, in general, not pure enough for the sacraments of any church, which requires *sterling* character as the condition of communion.

Besides, there are in every conscientious church a goodly number who both bear the image and breathe the spirit of Christ; who are walking humbly and circumspectly in the narrow way that leadeth to life; who are bearing their own crosses, and each other's burdens, well; and trying to live " as heirs together of the grace of life;" and these, we know, shall inherit heaven. We calculate on sitting down with them in the kingdom of God. Why not, then, sit down with *them* here, in humble anticipation of associating with them there? In no other way can we cultivate that *kind* of Christian fellowship which prevails in heaven, and which we expect to share and reciprocate through eternal ages. And, as the Saviour will be the grand centre of that fellowship, and of all the other felicities of heaven, why not use and enjoy the sacramental pledges of them now, as preludes of eventual communion with Him, and with all who are His? This would render the house of God, emphatically, the gate of heaven to us; for nothing is so like the bliss or the business of eternity as the joint celebration of redeeming love.

The HOLINESS, also, required and promoted by the house of God, renders it both an emblem and a pledge of heaven. There is far more similarity between the terms of communion in the church militant, and the terms of admittance into the church triumphant, than is usually noticed. It is, however, just as true that the unclean, the intemperate, and the dishonest, should be kept out, and cast out, of the church on earth, as that they shall not enter into the church in heaven. This general law is the same in both worlds. Nothing that defileth shall enter the gates of the New Jerusalem; and none who are immoral ought to be allowed to remain in the fellowship of Zion. "Purge out," says Paul, "the old leaven." 1 Cor. v. 7, 13.

Had this apostolic rule been acted upon, honestly and uniformly, there would have been less difficulty in proving that

> "The church on earth, and all the dead,
> But one communion make;"

for it requires but little candor, and less imagination, to regard a body of holy persons, as akin to "the spirits of just men made perfect." Holiness and heaven are ideas which naturally blend, and suggest each other. We never see an eminently holy man, without thinking of heaven. We feel as sure that he belongs to it, as we should if we saw an angel. How readily and vividly, therefore, would a holy church bring before our minds that glorious church which is without spot before the throne? Well, there are churches, which, to say the least, are not unholy. Their general character is pure and peaceable. Their moral worth gives them moral weight. Their watchfulness to keep out, and to cast out, unworthy communicants, entitles them (whatever name they bear) to the respect and gratitude of all who believe that the church should be a nursery for heaven.

Do we, then, belong to a holy church? If so, how useful and delightful its character may be to us! Let us look round from Sabbath to Sabbath, and especially on sacramental Sabbaths, upon our brethren and sisters in Christ, as our eternal companions in the kingdom of God. Let us not stop at the fact, that it is creditable and pleasing to be identified with them on earth. It is, indeed, so: but this is not all the truth. That moral excellence, and evangelical spirit, which render their fellowship so gratifying, render their glory sure; and, therefore, we ought, whilst worshipping with them, to anticipate that glory, and to treat them as the heirs of it. And they, also, will regard us in the same light, if they see any good reason for believing that the love of Christ constrains us to follow holiness.

It will, also, add much to our enjoyment of the sanctuary, if we pause for a moment, whenever our hearts are in their best frame, to say unto ourselves, " This, and more than this relish and rapture, will prevail for ever, when we exchange worlds. There will be no return to folly, and no relapse into formality, when we reach heaven. There, he that is holy will be holy still; and the beauty of his holiness remain as unchangeable as the immortality of his being."

And even when the frame of our minds is dull and earthly, the best thing we can do to quicken our relish for holiness is, to anticipate heaven. That, indeed, is not easily done, when the heart is not right with God. Then it seems presumption to cherish the hope of glory. If, however, we do not, and dare not, abandon that hope altogether, even then; if we still cling to it, although our soul "cleaveth to the dust," nothing is so likely to bring our spirit into harmony with it, as the distinct realization of the time, when we shall "bear the image of the heavenly," as fully as we now bear "the image of the earthy." Yes; the time, yea, the eternity, is coming, when it will be as impossible for our spirits to weary in well doing, or to lose their unction, as it is for angels to dislike heaven, or to distrust God. Thus, the due consideration of "what we shall be" hereafter, has a direct tendency to make and keep us what we ought to be here.

The mutual LOVE, also, which prevails in heaven, has its best emblems and exemplifications in the house of God. Domestic love embraces too narrow a circle, and social love is too much blended with self love, to be types of that attachment which, like the principle of gravitation linking star to star throughout the universe, however they differ in glory, links spirit to spirit throughout heaven, without partiality and without hypocrisy. There they love each other " for the truth's sake which dwelleth in them, and shall be in them;" and because God and the Lamb love them all with a perfect love.

It is only in the church that this principle is acted on, or recognized. And, if it be too little acted on there,—and, alas, it is so! still it has no power nor place in any other form of society. Cordial love to God and the Lamb, is no condition of membership, and no current claim for esteem, in any secular association of men. Neither political nor commercial bodies, as such, judge of men by their conformity to the image of God, nor by their love to the Saviour. Whilst, therefore, I would neither hide nor palliate the sad deficiency of brotherly love which prevails in our churches, I boldly maintain that nowhere else is there any semblance of *that* love which makes heaven so lovely. Love " for the truth's sake " is disowned or overlooked in all temporal confederations. Some of these may maintain religious tests; but, in general, real personal religion is no recommendation to office, and no plea for influence in the world. It is impossible, there, to learn the spirit, the motives, or the forms of that love, which will blend and bind all heaven in eternal harmony. Except by contrast, no one was ever led to think of heaven by the aspect or the spirit of any secular assembly. But, in a church, that deserves the name, let any number of new and real converts come forward, or any number of old converts evince a new measure of piety, and both will be welcomed and loved on the single ground of their love to Christ. An accession to the church in heaven could not be more sure of a cordial welcome from saints and angels, than true penitents may be here from all whose love is worth possessing. On all the hills of Zion, as on Mount Sion, there is joy over one sinner that repenteth. Unless, therefore, we exclude from *meetness* for the inheritance of the saints in light, the love which unites them, we must acknowledge that the house of God is the gate of heaven; for, nowhere else is there any public recognition of the grand principle which unites that general assembly. "Receive one another, even as Christ hath received you," is a lesson not to be learnt in the world.

Is this, then, a part of the meetness for heaven, that we are cultivating? Or, are we taking our *chance* of catching the spirit of celestial love at the gates of the New Jerusalem? Why not take our chance of becoming holy there, without following holiness here? We dare not hazard our souls on that experiment. All our ideas and hopes of heaven constrain us to follow holiness. Why? If because it is declared to be necessary, so also is brotherly love. "Whosoever hateth his brother is a murderer: and ye know that no murderer hath eternal life abiding in him. If a man say, I love God, and hateth his brother, he is a liar: for he that loveth not his brother whom he hath seen, how can he love God, whom he hath not seen? There is nothing said of holiness, more solemn, or heart-searching, or authoritative than this. And this is the law of the house of God, just because it is the gate of heaven. Love is no more left to be optional, or to be made a matter of convenience, than holiness is so. The one is as binding as the other; and both equally a part of meetness for heaven.

Now, it is by keeping the eternal love and

fellowship of the saints in light habitually before our minds, that we shall best grow in this grace of the Spirit. Nothing is so effectual in preventing and healing breaches amongst brethren, as the consideration that they will be cordial friends in heaven to all eternity. A moment of this thought makes us look foolish, and feel guilty, whenever we are conscious of an unchristian temper towards a fellow heir of eternal life. Even if he is much in fault, we dare not contemplate meeting him in glory, before we forgive him.

No. VIII.

ETERNITY REALIZED AT THE SACRAMENT.

WHATEVER may be the present state of our views or feelings in regard to the sacramental supper of the Lamb, our *first* approach to his table was unfeignedly and peculiarly solemn. This was the case, whether that approach was made in much hope, or in much fear; in joy, or in doubt. If hope predominated in our minds, it did so, as it reigns in the mind of a dying Christian, who is departing " in peace ; " —as solemnly as sweetly. It was as thoughtful and prayerful, as it was soothing. It was a hope " clothed with humility," and quivering with holy awe. Even if joy predominated, it, too, was emphatically " a holy joy." Tears, rather than words, were the chief expression of it. It was as retiring as it was intense. Solitude, not publicity, was its chosen element.

We were even jealous of that joy, because we felt ourselves to be utterly unworthy of it.

We remember all this well. We can never forget it, however often or much we have, since, failed to realize that state of mind. We partook of our first sacrament with much of that deep solemnity which pervades the spirit of a dying saint, when partaking of his *last* sacrament. And his solemnity is "very deep!" It both sanctions and sanctifies his application of the Saviour's words to his own case: "I will drink no more of the fruit of the vine, until that day that I drink it new, in the kingdom of God." Accordingly, whatever be the literal meaning of these words, or the prophetical meaning of the apocalyptic "marriage-supper of the Lamb," we admire and approve his touching transition of thought, from the last sacramental supper on earth, to his first celebration of the marriage-supper in heaven: it is, in his circumstances and spirit, so natural, appropriate, and beautiful! Indeed, this is just the way in which we wish to be exercised, when *our* last sacrament comes. We should so like!—to be able to enjoy it as the pledge and prelude of the heavenly feast: so like!—to be able to say to our friends, "I am going to drink of the fruit of the vine, new, in the kingdom of God." For, we feel that, whatever material imagery runs through such figurative language, we should not be misunderstood at that moment; and we cannot but think, that the calm and solemn utterance of such a good hope, when we are on the uttermost verge of eternity, would tend much to endear the sacrament to those members of our family who "keep the feast;" and to enforce its holy and sweet claims on those of them who neglect it.

Well; our last sacrament will come: it may come soon! And, should we know it to be our *last*, we shall feel it to be very solemn. We shall feel, as if *light* from eternity were the covering of the table; as if a *hand* from eternity set out and served the sacred emblems; as if a *voice* from eternity uttered the welcome, "Eat, O friends: drink, O beloved;" as if *echoes* from eternity repeated the closing hymn,

"'Tis done; the great transaction's done!"

Will it be thus? Ought it to be thus, at our last sacrament? If so, there may be something, there ought to be much, of this realizing sense of eternity, at every sacrament. Any one, even the next, may be our last.

But, however many "solemn feasts" may

be between us and the "marriage-supper of the Lamb" in heaven, each of them has the same connection with heaven as the last will have. And, as the last may, from our extreme weakness, or extreme pain, be any thing but a "time of refreshing," it becomes, yea, it behoves us, to try at the next, and at every subsequent sacrament, how much we can connect it with heaven and eternity. The mind cannot, indeed, throw itself, even by an effort, so far "within the veil," as the immediate prospect and pressure of death will throw it. We cannot force such glimpses of eternity, as the approach of death forces upon us. We cannot *command* that entire and intense concentration of spirit in the house of God, which is so natural, though inevitable, in the house of mourning, at the moment the mourning begins. There, and then, without effort, and even without intention, we find ourselves absorbed with eternal things. The departure of one spirit into the invisible world, displaces, for a time, this world, in all the spirits present. The unclothed soul cannot rise more rapidly to the throne of God, even if borne on angels' wings, than the thoughts and feelings of survivors rush into the realization of meeting God. Their spirits are "naked and open," too, before God, although in another sense: for, at this solemn moment they heed nothing, and hear nothing, of all that is " under the sun."

On such occasions, the soul asserts its own immortality, and springs at once into its own element, in spite of all the temporal considerations which may be around it. Neither grief nor gain can materialize it, for a time. Its freedom and force may not last long; but there is an immortal energy about them, for a little, that makes the body feel that its limits are too narrow, and its breathing too slow, for the full action of a fully *conscious* spirit.

When we come from such a scene to the first sacrament after it, this absorbing consciousness of our immortality, although softened and tranquillized by the interval, is yet so vital and vivid, that it gives to that sacrament much of the aspect of a last one. Deep thoughts of our own death, mingle with our sweetest recollections of the Saviour's death. We communicate for eternity. There is an *air* of eternity about the sanctuary, and about ourselves too. Our sympathising friends feel the "*unction*," as well as the weight, that is on our spirit. For it is not their sense of our *loss* alone, that so readily and fully harmonizes their looks and tones with our own, when they meet us for the first time, after we come from the house of mourning to the house of God. That holy and solemn awe which breathes in all their manner towards us, is chiefly derived *from* us. They feel that we have been so near the eternal world, that any thing not solemn, would be as unkind to our seriousness as to our sorrow. They know that we went so far down into " the swellings of Jordan," with the spirit which so recently passed through them, that they look as if they saw drops of the cold and dark waters still hanging upon us. And we, too, feel, however soothed or reconciled, that it would be a kind of sacrilege even to smile, for a time.

These familiar facts prove, not that it is possible, or even desirable, to communicate in this spirit always; but that it is possible, and therefore desirable, to cultivate so much of a realizing sense of eternity, that each sacrament may have an express reference to it. And this, each may have, as well the last, without at all overcasting or overstraining the mind. Our *first* did neither; and yet it was very solemn.

The form of these remarks is very defective, or the design of them is sadly misunderstood, if they seem to inculcate the necessity or the desirableness of an *habitual* awe on the spirit, equal to that we have just contemplated. The spirit could not sustain such a load, long. It would "fail" under the strain and pressure of habitual concentration. Indeed, any concentration of its thoughts and feelings, which would unfit us for the ordinary duties of life and godliness, is to be deprecated. We were not made, nor yet redeemed, for *thinking* only, nor for *feeling* only. Thinking deeply, for the sake of thought; or feeling deeply, for the sake of emotion, is oftener a "lust of the mind," than a grace of the Holy Spirit. And, in the case of that, almost, convulsive excitement, which is produced by the shock, or the fear, of death, there is little or no *religion* in it. It takes place, in almost all its forms and force, where there is no religion at all. Even some of our domestic animals, are overwhelmed by the loss of their young.

Nothing, therefore, can be farther from my design, than to represent "the power of godliness," as an overpowering emotion, or even as powerful excitement. Indeed, one grand feature of it is,—power *over* all excess both of thought and feeling. The foregoing references to our final sacrament, and to the first one after bereavement, are intended, therefore, not to bring up, at every sacrament, all the feelings peculiar to these extraordinary occasions; but to bring *out* of that chaos of feeling, the light of eternity which pervades it; and to embody that light in an orb, which shall shine as calmly, and constantly, and brightly, on the sacramental table, as the lamps of the temple shone on the altars of sacrifice and incense. For it is possible, and desirable, and safe, to have such an habitual sense of eternity, as shall render every sacrament a foretaste of the marriage-supper of the Lamb. Each is both intended and adapted to be so, by God; and, therefore, should be received as such by us.

In like manner, nothing is farther from my intention than to give a mystical, or superstitious, or undue importance to the act of communicating, or to the sacrament itself. Any thought, however profound, and any feeling, however spiritual, which *terminates* on the symbols or the ceremony, is far from blameless. The sacrament, and the sacramental act, are nothing, but as they bring the soul near to the Saviour, and bind it to holiness. Like the Bethel ladder, they are beautiful in their simplicity of form, and sublime in their suitableness of place; but it is *"the Lord standing above"* them, that is their real glory; as their tendency to lead to Him, is their real use. This must never be forgotten. We have done nothing in religion, and nothing that is truly spiritual, when we have broken bread, and drank wine, in the sanctuary; however deep may have been the silence, and however decorous the solemnity, with which this has been done; unless that deep silence was the expression of deep humility, and that solemnity the effect of communing with God and the Lamb.

We should never hesitate to acknowledge nor to proclaim this, whatever use some may make of the concession. It may be turned against the necessity of the sacrament. Those who deny the permanency of its obligation, as a Christian ordinance, may argue, that they can commune with God and the Saviour, as well without it. This is, however, but mere assertion, founded on gratuitous assumption; for, as they have never tried the experiment of communing with God *with* it, they are not qualified to judge. They are, of course, both competent and good judges of their own communion with God *without* it; but, certainly, not of our's *with* it. They are as ignorant of how far our enjoyment exceeds their own, as we are of how far their enjoyment falls short of ours. Perhaps, a *little* more ignorant; for we have some experience both of the kind and degree of fellowship with God, which is enjoyed without the sacrament: whereas they have none of the kind or the degree which is peculiar *with* it.

Having thus guarded against misunderstandings, let us look fairly and fully in the face of the question. How, and how much, may the light of eternity be brought and kept upon the holy sacrament? We have seen that death, and the fear of death, can actually enshrine it with much of the glory, and with more of the solemnities, of eternity. And we remember, that, when we have come from the tomb to the table, we have communicated in "a right spirit." And, as we felt then, and feel still, that we were not *too* serious, nor *too* prayerful, even then; we are bound by consistency, to meet the question,—How far can we communicate habitually for eternity?

Now, do not imagine nor suspect, that this question is intended or calculated, to bring in any *new* principle, or *new* feeling, into your sacramental devotion. Its real and sole design is, to purify that devotion, by making the usual train of thoughts and feelings flow more freely on the channels of eternity, and set in more directly to the shores of immortality.

And as, at each successive sacrament, we ourselves are nearer and nearer to the invisible world, it is, surely, neither unnatural nor unreasonable, that our reflections and emotions should advance in their intimacy with it. Our bodies are for ever growing liker and liker to the mortality that awaits them; and our spirits ought to assimilate more and more to the immortality that awaits them.

Now, it is not difficult to realize the *manner* in which we should celebrate the love of Christ in heaven. The moment we think of "sitting down" at the feast there, in the immediate and unveiled presence of the Master of the feast; and next to the spirits we love; and near to the whole "general assembly" of saints and angels,—we feel at once that we should take our place with great solemnity, and occupy it with holy awe, and employ it for holy purposes. Not a look nor motion would be out of *character* with the scene or the service. We should be afraid to glance even at the whole landscape of Paradise, lest it should divert us, for a moment, from gazing upon the Lamb in the midst of the throne, or from swelling the chorus of the new song. All levity, and listlessness, and vacancy, and the very appearance of them too, would be as much avoided as sleep or irreverence. And, is not more of this reverential manner as possible, as it is desirable, at the sacramental feast on earth? Would it not promote all the spiritual purposes of communicating, and improve its spirit too, to place ourselves, in thought, at the table above, until we felt that the table below was on " holy ground," and worthy of the most solemn deportment? This would prevent all postures, and motions, and looks, which tend to deaden our own minds, or to disturb others.

In like manner, it is not very difficult to realize the *spirit* in which we should " keep the feast" in heaven. We do, occasionally, catch a glimpse of the warm emotions which the first welcome into heaven, the first sight of heaven, the first access to the throne of heaven, will awaken! We have some conception of the mighty burst of mingled wonder, gratitude, and humility, which will be called forth, by finding ourselves there! Even our resolution is already taken, that no spirit who has preceded us at the throne, and none who follow us, shall be more humble or grateful. We are quite sure that we shall prostrate ourselves and our crowns, as low as the lowliest; and employ our harps as cordially and constantly, as any spirit in the general assembly of perfect spirits.

These intentions and anticipations are occasionally present to our minds, during our solitary walks, and when we are musing or praying in our closets. Even when surrounded by our families at home, fond hope will, now and then, dart off to heaven, with *them* in her arms, and go through all the glorious act of presenting them safe and spotless before the throne, with exceeding joy!

Thus we can, we do, realize " glorious things," at times, and in places, where there is not so much to suggest the idea of them, or to assist us in realizing them, as there is in the sanctuary and at the sacrament. Why not, then, before taking our place at the table of the Lord, place ourselves in thought at the throne of the Lord, until we see and feel the *kind* of penitence, and the *kind* of humility, and the *kind* of gratitude, and the *kind* of love, which becomes those who take " the cup of blessing" on earth, as the pledge of " the cup of salvation" in heaven? No process nor direction of thought would so readily improve " a right spirit," or correct a wrong spirit. Indeed, it is only by some process akin to this, that we can succeed in securing a sacramental spirit: for it will not be *forced*. All attempts to throw out vain thoughts, or to throw off bad feelings, by dint of mere effort, almost defeat themselves. These things can only be displaced by heavenly things. Whilst Abraham only "drove away the fowls" that alighted on his sacrifice, "an horror of great darkness" was upon him; but, when he saw the fire of heaven, like "a burning lamp," upon the altar, he was able to renew his covenant with God. So it is with us. Whilst we are merely *driving away* "the unclean birds," which haunt the cage of the heart, there is only hurry, or confusion, or pain of heart. We are almost glad to avoid thinking altogether, that we may not run the risk of falling into trains of vain thoughts. We sometimes suppress our very breathing, that we may suppress the wanderings of our minds; and we even try to create an utter vacuum in our spirit, in the hope that the Spirit of God will fill it with holy ideas and emotions.

Now, although these struggles between the flesh and the spirit, at the sacrament, tell a sad tale, and betray humiliating secrets, concerning both the neglect of due preparation, and the want of habitual watchfulness; they show, also, that we have much to learn on the subject of that "all diligence," by which the heart may be kept right with God. One part of that diligence is, the habit of looking at "the things which are eternal." They must be brought *into* our minds, if "the things which are temporal" are to be driven *out* of our minds, whilst we commemorate the death of Christ. And, how much easier and pleasanter it is, instead of a feverish or confused effort to be solemn and devout, just because we *ought* to be so, to have recourse, at once, to the contemplation of an eternity that can *make* us so! Eternal redemption—eternal love—eternal life,—are objects which cannot fail to dislodge vain thoughts, nor to quicken dull feelings, if any due measure of attention and prayer be given to them.

In like manner, it is not difficult to realize the *purpose* for which we should keep the feast in heaven. For, were it possible to pass within the vail of that temple "once every year," or even once in the course of our life, and to remain as long as the high-priest did in the holy of holies; and then to return to the earth, not at all unfitted for the ordinary duties of life, nor at all insensible to the real worth and claims of human affairs; we see, at a glance, that we should make all the enjoyment of this visit to the "third heavens" bear upon practical holiness for ever after. We feel, that, if it were put to us, whilst within the vail, what we should choose to bring down from heaven, as most useful on earth, and most conducive to promote our final meetness for " eternal inheritance," we should fix upon the grace which would enable us " to pass unspotted through the world." This, after having seen God's " holy hill," we should prefer to a crown of glory, or a harp of gold, when we had to *return* to the work and warfare of faith, in this world. Indeed, no fruit " of the tree of life, which is in the midst of the paradise of God," would be preferred to that, which would fortify us to do and endure the will of God well. Or, if we did feel any longing to bring down something, which should attract public notice by its splendor, or feed self-complacency by its singularity, we should blush for ourselves, and flee from the vain desire, " as from a serpent."

Now, even by this brief look at " eternal things," we have caught a glimpse of the practical purpose of sacramental communion, which is just as *sober*, as the point from which it is gained is fanciful. That which we would thus bring from the table in heaven, we ought to *seek*, chiefly, at the table on earth;—firmness to resist temptation, and fortitude to bear our trials.

At the hazard of being charged with repetition, but with the hope that it will not be "vain repetition," I renew my appeals on the subject of "brotherly love." The want or the weakness of this grace, is one great cause of the want of sensible enjoyment at the sacrament. Towards some, whom God loves, we have no love that is worth mentioning; and, towards others, we have hardly good-will. We have been offended, perhaps injured, by a few; and although we forgive, we do not forget; but take care that they shall know, if not feel too, that we *remember* them. Now, we could not remember them in this way, were their souls and our souls to meet at the marriage-supper of the Lamb, in heaven. There, we should feel as much ashamed of our former high spirit, as they would of their former mean spirit. Neither party could bear an apology nor a confession from the other, before the throne. The bare idea of recrimination, or even of mutual explanations, there, is intolerable! We feel, instinctively, that all unpleasant recollections would be for ever lost, in the rapture of meeting to part no more.

Now, although it is not necessary to bring all this heavenly temper to bear upon earthly fellowship, it is necessary that personal offences, which do not *unchristianize* the offender, should not subject him to unchristian treatment. He ought not to be treated as innocent, if he has done wrong; but, if the wrong do not *disprove* all his pretensions to piety, he must not be treated as an " alien." Consider! he may for ever sit *next* to you in heaven.

No. IX.

ETERNITY REALIZED AT HOME.

Both the manner and the degree in which the habits and happiness of domestic life may be improved by the mutual hope of eternal life, deserve the serious attention of all husbands and wives who are " heirs together of the grace of life." No fastidious delicacy, nor dread of singularity, should be allowed to prevent them from thinking or speaking of their eternal prospects, exactly as God has spoken. No length of time, during which we have been *silent* on this subject, should deter us from familiarizing ourselves with it. "The mighty God, the Lord, hath spoken," freely and frequently, upon it; and, as He never speaks without occasion, nor without design, on any subject, we may be sure that his reasons are weighty when he speaks of marriage.

Now, God has expressly said, that "marriage is honorable;" and, accordingly, he himself signally honors it, by making it the emblem of his own love to believers, and of their union to Him. "I am married unto thee," was the frequent and emphatic language of God to his ancient church. Nor is this emblem less employed in the case of the Christian church. Her union to Christ is represented as conjugal. Even in heaven, her name is "the Bride, the Lamb's wife. Thus signally does God honor the relationship, which he calls "honorable."

It may be criticism to say, "that it is the *poverty* of human language which gives rise to the use of such emblems." It is, however, sense, as well as piety, to say, that the riches of divine grace require the use of them. It may be philosophical to regard them as accommodations to the weakness of our minds. It is, however, wisdom to regard them as accommodated to the strength of redeeming love in the eternal mind. Such metaphors have, indeed, reasons in both our mental and moral weakness; but their chief reasons are in the manifold wisdom and grace of God. And one of them is—to exalt and endear the marriage union itself, by throwing around it the charms of a better paradise than that in which it originated. All the divine arrangements and declarations on the subject of marriage, have an express and splendid reference to ETERNITY. The conjugal union is made the emblem of all the grace which gives a title to eternal life, just that husbands and wives may live and love now, " as being heirs together of the grace of life." Their mutual hope of dwelling together in heaven, is made the grand motive and rule of their dwelling together in harmony on earth. This strong and lovely motive is in nowise weakened or dimmed by the fact, that " in heaven they neither marry nor are given in marriage." The same high authority which reveals this fact, declares that " they are equal unto the angels ;" a consideration quite sufficient to inspire the most exalted expectations of mutual recognition and enjoyment. Angels are not unacquainted with, nor indifferent to, each other. Both their love and fellowship are perfect. It is impossible to form a higher or a holier idea of mutual happiness, than their union and communion before the throne ; and, therefore, to be " equal unto the angels" in heaven, is the very perfection of social felicity and personal glory.

It is, then, the revealed fact, that pious

husbands and wives shall be like the angels of God in heaven. This is our joint heritage there, who are joint heirs of salvation here. "Equal unto the angels!"—Surely, this prospect deserves to be greeted with something more grave than a *smile*. It is not visionary nor fanciful. It is a leading and everlasting feature of the heavenly constitution. It is an actual and prominent part of that "life and immortality, which Jesus Christ brought to light, through the gospel;" and, therefore, any appearance of levity or indifference towards it, is inconsistent with our habitual veneration for our Lord and Saviour, as "the faithful and true witness." There is, I am aware, no disrespect, towards Him or His word, intended, by the smile which usually awaits this subject. A tear would, however, be a more appropriate tribute to the *moral* aspect of the subject; for, how few partners act up to the prospect of being eternally "equal unto the angels?" Even the most amiable and exemplary are not, always, to each other, exactly "that manner of persons" which *they* ought to be, and might be, who "look for such things" as angelic union and communion in heaven. And, if those who live and love most as heirs together of the grace of life, feel reproved by this prospect, what a reproof it administers to those who neither live nor love so well, as even some do who make no pretensions to religion? Their mutual hope of eternal harmony cannot be very bright, who live in discord. The idea of being for ever, or even ever, like the angels of God in heaven, cannot occur often to the contentious, or the capricious. It does not occur so often to the considerate and affectionate, as it ought to do.

This is held to be a very delicate subject. Why it should be reckoned so, is not very evident. Domestic habits and tempers are treated with equal freedom and frequency by the Scriptures; and it is matter of universal experience, although not of general acknowledgment, that domestic happiness depends more upon *temper* than upon talents or wealth. Were, however, the proverb, that " temper is every thing," to come into general use, it could not create all the good temper which domestic happiness requires. It would, of course, be very useful, as a check upon passion and peevishness; but there is no *charm* in it, to sanctify or soften the heart. It is a good law in itself, but it brings with it no new *power* of obedience. This, however, all the Christian laws of domestic life do bring with them. They inspire to the duties they prescribe.

This is a peculiarity of Christianity which is not sufficiently appreciated or noticed. There is a delicacy, a tenderness, "a small, still voice," in the family code of the New Testament, which is heart-touching; and thus transforming in its sweet influence. Look and listen again to that great commandment, upon which all "the law of the house" hangs; "Dwell, as being heirs together of the grace of life." This appeal is irresistible, when fairly weighed. There is a point, a charm, an indescribable something, about the letter and spirit of it, which tells more than ten thousand prudential or authoritative maxims could. The moment it is proposed as a rule to joint heirs of salvation, it is approved by them; and, as soon as it is considered, it appears, like a summer rainbow, a bow of peace, encircling and enshrining the whole round of domestic duties.

Illustration is, however, more wanted than eulogium, on this subject. Now, it deserves our special notice, that God, in giving laws to believing partners, never urges mutual love or peace by the prospect of *death*. We are, indeed, "heirs together" of the sentence of death;

and there is much in our mutual mortality to commend and enforce mutual kindness. We cannot live together long. The term of our union may be very short. And, as unkindness and neglect are fearfully avenged, by the upbraidings of conscience, when death does come, we do well to prepare a good conscience for the solemn occasion. Death is not allowed, however, to appear at all in the appeal which God makes to our hearts on behalf of the domestic virtues. The whole motive is drawn from eternal life; and is so "full of glory," that it fills up "the valley of the shadow of death" with brightness. We must, indeed, die, in order to inherit the kingdom of God; but, still, it is the kingdom of God, and not the kingdom of death, which is placed and kept before our minds.

This is not by accident, nor without design. The Searcher of hearts, who knoweth our frame, knows that we, of all persons, are most averse to contemplate death; and, therefore, in order that we may have no excuse for not thinking of heaven, He founds his appeals to us, not on our mortality, but entirely on our immortality; that, thus, death might be "swallowed up in victory." This is as wise as it is kind. It is the only way to conquer *parental* fears of death.

Moral maxims, however just, and direct warnings, however solemn, could not win us to the habitual consideration of our latter end, whilst our children are young. The degree of warning, that would compel us to number our days, would soon shorten our days, or unfit us for our duties; and thus defeat its own purpose. It is not, therefore, by warnings, nor by plying us with motives, derived from the shortness of life, or the solemnity of death, that God enforces our conjugal and parental duties. We are not brought " unto the mount that burned with fire; nor unto blackness and darkness and tempest; nor unto the sound of a trumpet," to hear the law of our mortality, or the law of our relationship; but we are brought to hear both sounding from " Mount Sion," the city of the living God, the heavenly Jerusalem; where " an innumerable company of angels" await our coming; and Jesus, the Mediator of the new covenant, preserves our prepared place for us. Truly our law, Christian parents! is " ordained by angels in the hand of a Mediator."

Were these facts as familiar to us as they are scriptural, we could not be so much in bondage to the fear of death, nor so silent about our hope of heaven. But they are not familiar; and the consequence is, there is little or no sweet counsel between husbands and wives on the subject. In general, heaven is almost as seldom realized or referred to as death. So unusual is any conversation on the point, that even a question about heaven, unless a *curious* one, would be reckoned an omen or foreboding of death, rather than a symptom of heavenly-mindedness. There are very few husbands or wives, who would not be more *startled* than gratified, by an attempt, on either side, to draw on a serious conversation about their mutual prospects for eternity. Even the discovery, or the suspicion, that the thoughts of either party were dwelling much upon heaven, would be interpreted into a sign that that party was "not long for this world." Thus the manifestation of heavenly-mindedness is rather dreaded than desired, even by pious partners; because they have fallen into the habit of regarding it as the forerunner of death.

And, is it not so? Is it not become almost proverbial to say, of those who begin to dwell much on heavenly things, "*that they are too ripe for glory, to be long here.*" And do not observation and experience, thus, give some countenance to the suspicion? I answer, at once,—none at all. The facts on which such questions are founded, are gathered from wrong quarters. They occur amongst aged, or very delicate Christians, whose many infirmities cannot be well sustained without much of the hope of eternal life; and, therefore, such facts prove nothing that is really applicable to the great majority of married believers. Wherever heavenly-mindedness seems an *omen* of approaching death, there are other omens indicating and hastening that approach. It is, therefore, not fair, to attribute an ominous character or aspect to the habit of looking to the things which are " unseen and eternal." Paul's confidence of life was strongest, at the very time when his heavenly-mindedness was the greatest. " I have a desire to depart, and to be with Christ; which is far better. Nevertheless, to abide in the flesh is more needful for you. And, having this confidence, I know that I shall abide and continue with you all, for your furtherance and joy of faith," Phil. i. 23. This case, although apostolic, is not unapplicable to Christian parents. Whilst God sees it to be really " more needful," for the sake of our children, that we should " abide" with them, the cultivation of a " desire to depart and to be with Christ," will no more hasten our departure than it did Paul's; but will, in fact, best qualify us for the " furtherance" of our children, in whatever is good for them. Besides, the natural tendency of that heavenly-mindedness which God inculcates, is, to promote health, and to prolong life. A hope full of immortality, is full of tranquillity and cheerfulness; and thus favorable to the body as well as to the mind. "What man is he that desireth life, and loveth many days, that he may see good?" Every pious husband. Then, " ye husbands, dwell with your wives, according to knowledge, giving honor unto the wife, as unto the weaker vessel, and as being heirs together of the grace of life. Likewise, ye wives, be in subjection to your own husbands; and let your adorning be, the hidden man of the heart, in the incorruptibility of a meek and quiet spirit,—which is, in the sight of God, of great price." Ye are both to be "equal unto the angels" in heaven; be not, therefore, *unlike* them, whilst you remain on earth.

"This view of the matter," it may be said, " is certainly very pleasing; but, as the hope of eternal life is not common nor constant, even amongst truly pious partners, how can it become a general principle of feeling or conduct?" Now, I readily grant, that if it were brought forward to set aside the use of other revealed principles or rules of domestic life, this would be a formidable objection. It is, however, advanced here, as it is in the Word of God, not to supersede any divine law, or natural affection, but to hallow all the former, and to sanctify all the latter. And, surely, if neither the frequent weakness, nor yet the occasional absence of the hope of eternal life, is found to set aside the use of our ordinary motives, the predominance of that hope is not likely to do so. If many good principles remain firm without much of it, more of it, is not calculated to relax them.

It is, however, very much doubted, whether such an habitual hope of heaven, as would habitually influence domestic life, be attainable by the generality of godly parents and partners. Many of both are quite of opinion that, whilst they have so little leisure, and so much care, they cannot reach the privilege of reading their

> " Title clear,
> To mansions in the skies."

And in this way we all reason, more or less. Indeed, it is with considerable difficulty that any one learns to suspect, even in secret, the hollowness of such reasoning; it is so plausible in appearance. Nothing seems more natural, or likely to be true, than that much time and little worldly care must be necessary, in order to acquire a bright and abiding hope of heaven. Nothing, however, is more *untrue* than this natural supposition. All the oracles of God contradict it; and no wonder! Our's is not a world in which much leisure time can be commanded; nor in which cares can be avoided; and, therefore, the gospel would ill accredit its own name or pretensions, if the hope of eternal life, which is its first promise, as well as its final reward, could not be enjoyed by those believers who have much to do and endure. The gospel is, therefore, misunderstood, so far, by all who imagine that their public duties, or their domestic cares, place them afar off from a lively hope of glory. It is just because we have so much to do and to suffer, as well as because it cannot be merited, that eternal life is the free gift, and the faithful promise of God, to believers; so that what we put forward as our reason for not venturing to cherish the hope of heaven, is actually one of God's reasons for making it as free as it is fair. Unless, therefore, a believing husband is doing something in his business, that is wrong; or his believing wife doing something in her family, that is imprudent; why should they not abound in hope? Their duties warrant, not forbid it. Their ultimate design in doing so much for their children is, that they too may choose the way to heaven: and, therefore, it would be *strange*, indeed, if such parental efforts were hinderances to parental anticipations of heaven. Those who regard family duties in this strange light, must have very unscriptural notions of both godliness and glory. There is, however, quite as much of that holiness, which constitutes *meetness* " for the inheritance of the saints," in providing for and bringing up a family in the fear of God, as in any other virtue of Christian character.

All these distinctions and explanations will not, however, remove the difficulty we naturally feel, unless we understand the gospel itself well. The pious husband or wife, who does not believe that " he that believeth in Christ *hath* eternal life," will not be able to keep up the hope of heaven. It will be thrown down or dimmed by every accident, and by all the fluctuations of their spirits and feelings. Indeed, it will *fall* down of itself, until it take its final stand on the promise of God through Jesus Christ. Now, he has promised eternal life unto them who rely on the cross for a holy salvation; and, therefore, it is just as much our duty to take the full comfort of the promise, as it is to give the cross our full confidence. Not even the plagues of our hearts, which we so often feel, and so deeply lament, must be allowed to prevent this duty of hoping unto the end. Giving up hope is, in fact, giving them head. If Satan succeed in his efforts to make us afraid of cherishing a good hope through grace, we shall soon settle into a worse frame than any we now deplore. The more, therefore, that we feel and fear the plagues of our hearts, the more reason we have to cling both to the cross and the crown; for all that is bad will only become worse, if we lose or lessen our hold upon either.

If these hints throw any light on the general subject of this Essay, they now warrant the question—why should not mutual heirs of the grace of life speak freely and frequently to each other of their eternal prospects? These prospects are not gloomy in their aspect, nor precarious in their tenure. It is true,

> " Death like a narrow sea divides
> That heavenly land from ours;"

but that sea is both bridged and brilliant to us, with the great and precious promises. Or, if we cannot yet realize it in this light, *silence* is not the best way to surmount our fears of death. These, like other fears, strengthen by concealment, and lessen by disclosure. Why not, then, discuss them as well as we do others? Why so much reserve, and shame, and timidity, on the subject of our mutual immortality? We are not indifferent to each other's final safety. Neither of us could bear the idea of *parting* in silence. Whichever may be the survivor, the utterance of a good hope will be anxiously looked for then. Consider this: we may be *unable* to utter the wished for " All is well," on our death bed. And, therefore, if we prolong our present silence, we are risking each other's comfort, at a moment when there is no such balm to the widowed and the wounded heart, as is the dying assurance of peace. O! let not the flow of that healing balm depend upon the vicissitudes of mortal pain! Let it drop in the garden of home now, and be treasured up "against that day."

Still, we shrink from *speaking* " as being heirs together of the grace of life." Why is this? Are we *not* joint heirs of salvation? Do we "stand in doubt" of each other? If not, what are we afraid of? Say not, "who must begin this unusual kind of communion?" Any *formal* effort to introduce it would prevent it. It must not be attempted as a task. Whoever is the first to break the ice on this subject, must not *seem* to be conscious that there is any ice to break. Family prayer is the best medium for introducing family hopes. The regular introduction, and the gradual amplification, of the apostolic thanksgiving, 1 Pet. i. 3, in prayer, would pave the way for conversation. For, what we often and openly united to say unto God, we should soon be able to say unto each other.

These remarks proceed on the assumption, that God is favorable to the domestic happiness of them who fear him, and solicitous to promote it. And this is the revealed fact. He looks with no unfriendly or jealous eye upon a happy home; nor considers time mis-spent, or religion misapplied, in multiplying *in-door* comforts. The family bliss which he breaks up so often by the strokes of his providence, and of which we are in the habit of saying, " it is too good to last long," is not the happiness now referred to. It is of life, health, and temporal prosperity, we speak thus; and these are precarious in every family, however the heads of it may feel or act together. No maxim, however good or well applied, can secure exemption from all domestic calamity. But the happiness which depends on mutual love, mutual tenderness, and mutual confidence, may be secured by living together as joint heirs of eternal life.

Now, there must be some favorable light in which pious husbands and wives view each other; and some leading reason to influence their mutual conduct; and, therefore, the most *endearing* light, and the *strongest* reason, should be frequently, indeed habitually, before their minds. And, what so endearing and dignifying as being called FELLOW-HEIRS of salvation? It is not under-rating any personal or relative charm, on either side, to affirm, that "a good hope through grace" eclipses them all; and is the best, indeed the only, permanent security, of all that is moral or amiable in the character. It ought, therefore, to be often referred to, and always acted upon, as the chief endearment of domestic life. But, is there not reason to fear, that it is too seldom and slightly noticed, even by pious partners? It is not intended to insinuate, by this question, that they are insensible to the value or the charm of each other's piety. No; they never think of it without pleasure and gratitude. But it may be questioned, whether we think of it so often as it deserves and demands. For, what is the fact, when husband and wife are possessors of "like precious faith?" They are warranted to reflect thus: "the object of my choice is chosen of God; is one for whom the Lamb died, and ever lives to intercede; one enlightened and renewed by the Holy Spirit; one to whom angels minister on earth, and for whom a crown of glory is laid up in heaven!" This is nothing more than the fact, translated into language: but, what a different effect this view of it has upon the heart, compared with the common-place emotion excited by the reflection,—he is a *good man*—she is a *good woman?* Even the more spirited reflection, " he or she is a *Christian*, if ever there was one," is not so inspiring as viewing each other as heirs together of the grace of life. The consideration, in this sublime form, carries away the mind at once to the grace of the Father in adopting; to the love of the Son in redeeming; to the power of the Spirit in converting the persons; and thus raises them, in each other's estimation, to a rank and importance equally high and holy! And while they realize each other's state before God, in this glorious light, what will they not *do* and *suffer* for each other? The bright consciousness of being "one in Christ Jesus," would not dim its lustre by an unkind word or look. Caprice, peevishness, and all the natural ebullitions of temper, if they should at times rush to the lips, would rush back, ashamed of themselves, as unseemly, and inconsistent with the mutual hope of eternal life.

Now, if the ordinary ties and attractions and endearments of domestic life, often fail to maintain uniform kindness and harmony—if even vague and occasional views of each other, as Christians, fail to carry husband and wife *calmly* through the duties and trials of home; and if the higher view would evidently have a happier influence, both duty and interest call for an immediate attention to the apostolic maxim—" Dwell, as being heirs together of the grace of life."

The maxim is equally important on other accounts. It is the only principle on which husband and wife can imbibe, or maintain the spirit of *Christian fellowship*. Now a free interchange of spiritual joys and sorrows is a rare thing in domestic life. There is often far more reserve, silence, and timidity, between man and wife, on this subject, than between each of them and their pious friends. Ministers often know more of the mind of both, than *they* know of each other's experience. And this happens where there is no want of mutual confidence; even where the parties think highly of each other's piety. But, having never ventured to unbosom themselves freely upon this one point, the state of their souls before God becomes almost an inviolate *secret* at home. They thus suffer and enjoy in silence; although they have no particular reason for being silent, except that they cannot break through the habit of reserve. This is one of the bad effects of overlooking the apostolic maxim at the outset of domestic life: communion of spirit is prevented by the neglect. There may be fellowship of opinion—fellowship of taste, maintained by an interchange of sentiment about books and sermons and ministers: but nothing will secure fellowship of *spirit*, between man and wife, but the habit of realizing and treating each other as joint heirs with Christ. And were they, on this principle, to speak freely to each other, both when all is well, and when all is wrong within, and to consult and console as fellow-heirs of salvation, the mutual benefit would be incalculable. Accordingly, the occasional instances, when reserve has been thrown off, or forced off, during the prospect of death, or the pressure of calamity, can never be forgotten by either party. The bright glimpses which they then gave each other of their hopes, are fixed stars in their memory. The secret, although only whispered, remains an everlasting music in each mind. Now, why is it not fully disclosed, and habitually reciprocated, that their "joy might be full?"

The bearings of this maxim upon the character and success of *parental instruction*, deserves special notice. For, how can religion be endeared to children by formal lessons, if there be no familiarity between parents in speaking of its hopes and comforts as their own? What charm or excellence can it obtain youthful credit for, if parents say nothing of the positive benefit which they themselves derive from it? Our children hear us speak freely and frequently of whatever else interests us deeply; and we feel it to be a sacred duty to prove to them, from the case of *others*, the value and necessity of piety: but, why not prove this to them from *our own* case and experience? This appeal would be more powerful. For, parents living and conversing together as joint heirs of eternal life, would thus give an effect to domestic instruction, which, as it could only be exceeded by the work of the Eternal Spirit, would be likely to secure his blessing.

Domestic *afflictions* likewise call for the use of this maxim. We are all liable to interruptions of health; and when they are long, fatiguing, and expensive, ordinary motives will not maintain that uniform patience, tenderness, and attentions, which are so requisite. But he, or she, who ministers to an heir, a joint heir of glory, will not weary in well-doing. That is a charm which, by not decaying itself, preserves from decay all the kindly feelings of nature and grace; and makes the watcher in the solitary sick chamber feel akin to the angels of God; "for, are they not all ministering spirits to the heirs of salvation?" The task of long watching and much serving may seem intolerable to others, who think of the object less as an heir of glory than as a *burden;* but, in the former light, it is watching the polishing of a "living stone," destined for a high place in the temple of God; watching the culminating of a star which is to differ from other stars in glory; watching the refining of gold that is to form part of the mediatorial crown.

No. X

CHRIST, THE GLORY OF ETERNITY.

Were there nothing else to prove the Divinity of the Saviour, but the degree in which the happiness of heaven is represented, as flowing from his presence and glory—that one fact is fatal to Socinianism, and to every system which makes the Son inferior to the Father. It is especially fatal to the theory of the mere humanity of the Saviour; for a mere man, however highly endowed or well disposed, could not render himself the *companion*, even, of the countless myriads who shall inherit heaven; much less could he be to each and to all the heirs of glory the eternal source and centre of their happiness. Such, however, the Lamb, in common "with God," is expressly and uniformly declared to be. To the Son, as much as to the Father, is ascribed the eternal absence of all pain in heaven.

GLORY OF ETERNITY. 181

"They shall hunger no more, neither thirst any more; neither shall the sun light on them, nor any heat: For the Lamb which is in the midst of the throne shall feed them, and shall lead them to living fountains of waters; and God shall wipe away all tears from their eyes." The absence of all darkness, mental and moral, is traced to the same source. " The glory of God did lighten it; and the Lamb is the light thereof; for there shall be no night there."

In literal accordance with this view of heaven, the Saviour, in his great intercessory prayer, addressed the Father thus,—"I will that they also whom thou hast given me, be with me where I am, that they may behold my glory." Thus also he spoke to his disciples, "If I go and prepare a place for you, I will come again, and receive you to myself; that where I am, there ye may be also." Thus Paul, also, summed up the bliss and glory which he anticipated in heaven,—"I desire to depart, and to be with Christ; which is far better." And, "to be forever with the Lord," is the apostolic form of embracing and embodying all the exceeding and eternal weight of glory. Now all this is utterly incompatible with the theory of a *finite* Saviour. The mere man—of Unitarianism; and the incarnate angel of Arianism, are equally unfit to be Jehovah's "FELLOW," in the mighty work of filling all heaven with everlasting joy and glory. He who is "equal with God," in the communication of that bliss, must be equal with God in his essence and resources. No finite being could so *universalize* his attentions amongst such myriads, as to gratify them all alike, even if his attentions were capable of perfecting their enjoyment.

Were there, therefore, only the legitimate inferences deducible from the single fact, that God and the Lamb are equally the revealed source and centre of the eternal bliss of heaven, I, as a believer in immortality, should feel bound, by reason and common sense, to reject both the Unitarian and the Arian view of Christ; just because such a Christ could not be, in common with the Father, the glory of such a heaven. I might not, indeed, be able to infer so much from the fact of his companionship with God in this matter, as I now *know* from express revelation; but I should be compelled to infer from it—or, rather, I could not shut my eyes to the natural inferences which emanate from it, like light from the sun,—that Jesus must be more than man, and higher than angels. In a word, it is Trinitarianism only, that furnishes a satisfactory explanation of the fact just stated; and that fact is so interesting, that it deserves the chief place in all our meditations on eternal glory.

With what sublime simplicity and brevity Paul sums up the bliss of heaven: "so shall we be forever with the Lord." It would be much to "be forever with" any one of the angels, in any part of heaven, however remote from the throne of God and the Lamb. It would be much to "be forever with" any one of the saints, even if not within the sight or the sound of the "general assembly" before the throne. It would be much to "be for ever" *alone* on the most distant hill of immortality. It would be much to "be for ever" *any where*, out of hell. What, then, must it be, to "be for ever with the Lord?"

When you think of hell, and realize, only for a moment, the bare idea of being "for ever with" Satan and his angels; "for ever with" all the impure and impenitent spirits in the universe, you feel, through all your soul, that even eternal solitude in any other spot of the universe, would be an unspeakable mercy. You are not only ready to say, "I had rather be a door-keeper" of the house of God in heaven, for ever, "than dwell in the tents of wickedness;" but you are ready to say, I had rather spend my eternity alone, even on the very shore of the "great gulph" which divides heaven and hell, if I were allowed to be on its *heavenly* side; than be free from torment on its infernal side; because, on the side next to heaven, I should, at least, escape the contamination of hell. O, yes; "Gather not my soul with sinners" for ever, wherever else it may be placed. Let me rather dwell for ever on the most distant and desolate star in space; or hover for ever through the gloom of starless infinity, eternally alone, than dwell where spirits are "unholy still, and filthy still."

It is, then, the sober fact, that any place out of hell, and any condition not unholy, are infinitely preferable to the wrath to come. Any of the imaginary conditions we have glanced at, we would gladly accept, rather than dwell with apostate and despairing spirits; even if there were no "devouring fire" in their everlasting prison. O, yes; let the soul only "*escape*" from that society and scene; and wherever it might wing its way in the regions of immensity; whether on, or beyond, the utmost limits of creation, it would for ever "sing of mercy," and say, at every spot where it paused, "the lines are fallen to me in pleasant places, and

GLORY OF ETERNITY. 185

I have a goodly heritage," although not in heaven!

All this is, happily for believers! impossible. It is not, however, improper, nor imprudent, to indulge the supposition, for the purpose of preparing ourselves to form a due estimate of heaven. Now, if eternal solitude would be endurable, even if in the vacant spaces of infinity, what must be the bliss of eternal society, around the throne of God and the Lamb? If to be for ever with *one* angel or saint, at the very farthest "borders of Emmanuel's land," would be "worthy of all acceptation," what will it be to be for ever with the "innumerable company of angels," and with all "the spirits of just men made perfect?" If to be a door-keeper of the heavenly temple would be joy unspeakable; what must be the joy of being "made kings and priests unto God?" And, if to be for ever with any one in heaven, would be certain and sublime happiness; what must be the certainty and sublimity of being "for ever with the Lord?" "FOR EVER WITH THE LORD!" There is no idea of heaven dearer to the followers of Christ, than this. All our other ideas of it, even the fondest of them, culminate and centre in seeing and being with the Saviour. Even the sweet hope of re-union with the spirits we love most, is sweetest in the form of joining them, to cast our crowns at his feet together. We feel that however high natural love may swell then, the only effect of it will be to swell higher the song, " unto Him that loved us, and washed us in his own blood, be glory for ever." Thus, husbands and wives, parents and children, will especially feel, when they meet before the throne; and, just in proportion to the joy of that meeting, will be the attention, and the gratitude, and the love, it will concentrate upon the Lamb, slain for *them!*

In like manner, all the joys and glories of heaven will, and must, have a similar influence on all the redeemed; because the whole church being equally indebted to Christ for heaven, the more glorious heaven is, the more grateful they must be to Him. "Whom have I in heaven but thee!" is an exclamation which nothing there will stop or lessen, even when all that is within the vail is as visible as it is eternal. For, as neither the splendor of daylight, nor the softness of moonlight diverts our thoughts from the luminaries which emit them; but rather fixes our attention on the sun that rules by day, and the moon that rules by night; so neither the personal nor the relative enjoyments of heaven, however manifold or entrancing, can have any other tendency than to endear the Saviour. There is, therefore, as much sound logic, as sublime poetry, in that stanza,—

> " Millions of years my wondering eyes
> Shall o'er his beauties rove ;
> And endless ages I'll adore
> The glories of his love ! "

Communion of spirit, with the very " Morning stars of the angelic hierarchy, will not prevent this admiration of the Saviour, even when they sing together from all their orbits, the wonders of creation ; and explain from all their experience, the mysteries of Providence. Indeed, every note of their " descant on creation," will naturally, and must inevitably, lead our minds to Christ;—" for by Him were all things created, visible and invisible;" so that the more the glories of the material universe are shown or celebrated in heaven, the more we shall turn to the Son, saying, with the Father, " Thou, Lord, in the beginning, didst lay the foundations of the earth; and the heavens are the works of thy hands." And, upon the same principle, if angels rehearse to us the history of every providential event, over which they sang " Hallelujah;" and even if the Eternal Spirit should solve the mystery of all these events, as they record them, the vast and varied theme will only, can only, increase our love to Him, whose incarnation and atonement were prepared for by the Old Testament series of these events, and rewarded by the New Testament series of providences. For, however the philosophy of nature and history may divert the mind from Christ crucified here, it will not do so there. Creation and providence, when seen in the light of eternity, will be as full of Christ, and lead as directly to Christ, as the Bible does now. As to Him, "all the prophets" give witness here; so there, every star visible from the heaven of heavens, will, like the star of Bethlehem, point to Him: and, as he is "all, and all, and Head over all things," in revelation; so, when all that infinity embraces, and all that eternity will explain, is as familiar as the flowers of the field now are, Jesus will still be all and all, and head over all, in heaven. "He must increase" for ever, however the arcana of the works of creation, and the workings of providence are laid open; and whatever be the glory of the prospects which shall dawn on the Church, when she is presented complete and spotless to the Father.

And, if the universe of being, in all its history and mystery unvailed, will be unable to divert the mind from the adoration or the admiration of the Lamb of God, it is needless to say, that no personal, or family, or social interest, will be able to do so. Whatever intimacies may be renewed or formed throughout the general assembly; and whatever delight may be derived from fellowship with angels of all orders, and saints of all ages; and whatever the degree of this holy intercourse may be, the direct tendency of the whole must be to exalt and endear the Saviour; because He is the direct *source* of the felicity.

It is, therefore, worthy of special attention, at this point of the argument, that it is by no arbitrary arrangement that the LAMB is the glory of heaven. He is not so, because he is appointed to be so; but he has been appointed because he *deserves* to be so. The Father has placed him only where the church would have placed him, of her own accord, if left to her own choice.

In like manner, it is not chiefly because it is law or duty, that the hearts and harps of all the redeemed will turn with adoring gratitude to the Redeemer; but because it is *natural* that they should thus centre upon Him, in common with the Father and the Holy Spirit. He would be enthroned with them in every heart, even if he were not "in the midst" of the eternal throne with them already; and, were there no legislative claim upon the love or gratitude of the church, she would continue the "new song," in all its compass and melody, without weariness for ever.

Such being the sober facts of the case, it is easy to see how all that will be known of the Father and the Spirit, however much it may be, must have the effect of endearing the Son. It is demonstrable, that the more God is unveiled, the more the Lamb will be admired. Indeed, the manifestation of the Father's glory, however full and clear, must manifest the glory of the Son, in the same proportion: for, He being "the brightness" of that glory, the brighter it shines, the more glorious he will appear. And, in like manner, the more the *person* of God is seen face to face, the more will the dignity of the Saviour be disclosed; because, He being "the express image" of that person, its manifestation will be his also.

This, although a delicate, is a delightful subject. We expect, or desire, to see much, and to understand more, of the divine nature. Our present ideas of it are rather dazzling, than distinct. We are even afraid to embody our conceptions of it; and shrink from stamping it with locality or shape. Even our conception of it is rather an emotion, than an image. No wonder, therefore, if we anticipate much from seeing God " as he is!" But, even this great sight will in nowise divert or divide our attention or attachment from the Saviour. No; when the veil drops, however far it descend, and however full may be the disclosure of godhead, all the bearings of this beatific vision, on Christ, will be the demonstration that " in Him dwelleth all the fullness of the godhead bodily." As he said on earth, " he that hath seen me hath seen the Father also;" so, when the Father shall show himself face to face in heaven, it will be in effect, saying, " he that hath seen me hath seen the Son also."

Nor is this all the tendency of the manifestation. Every ray of its glory, whilst it will unveil the essential glory of the Lamb, will also invest his cross with new and heightened attractions; and thus promote and prolong for ever the celebration of his atonement. For, the more that is shown of the majesty, the holiness, the justice, and the love of God, the more will and must the wonders of the cross be admired, and the manifold wisdom of it be studied by all the redeemed.

This line of argument is equally applicable

to the manifestation of the person and glory of the Eternal Spirit. Nothing that he does now in sanctifying or consoling the church, diverts or divides her attention from the Saviour; but the whole bearing of spiritual operations and influences, is to " glorify Christ." Now, if this be their direct tendency, whilst they are but partially understood, and but inadequately appreciated, it is self-evident that they can have no different effect, when they are all fully estimated in heaven. No; when all the agency of the Holy Spirit, and all the holy results of it are familiar, it will just, like the beatific vision of the Father's person and glory, enshrine the Lamb slain with proportionate effulgence.

Thus all that we know or can anticipate of heaven, tends only to confirm the revealed fact, that to " be ever with the Lord," is the very *substance* of eternal happiness. Being " ever with " the Father and the Holy Spirit, will just *demonstrate* this fact. For, let it never be forgotten, that it is the atoning work of the Son, which has brought out, into such full and harmonious display, the glories of the divine nature and character. Through no other medium could they have been so perfectly manifested. Whatever, therefore, be the degree in which God is glorified by the full development of his perfections, the Lamb furnished both the opportunity and the medium of it; and, therefore, when it is fullest and fairest, the Lamb must still be the mirror in which it shines.

Having thus endeavored to realize some of the chief joys of being with the Lord, it will not be imprudent nor unprofitable to glance at the pleasures which must spring from witnessing his present *offices*, in heaven. We now think of his INTERCESSION with delight. We shall soon *see* how it is conducted. And, whatever be the manner or the spirit in which he intercedes, both will throw back our thoughts upon the lowness of our past and present estimate of it. Nothing, perhaps, will deepen our humility in heaven, more than the remembrance of our reluctance to pray, when we see how the Father " waiteth to be gracious; " and how the Son " ever liveth to intercede." We shall judge impartially then, how they ought to pray, whom we have left on earth; and, in thus judging of their duty, we shall, with all the reason and conscience of our perfected spirits, condemn the formality and coldness which so often marked our own devotion. Only think!—

what we must feel when we first see the Saviour rise before the throne to intercede for those whom we have left? It is not necessary, in order to realize the effect of this act on our minds, that we should assist our thoughts now by the material imagery of a "golden censer," or of "much incense." No; the bare idea, that he "appears in the presence of God for" his people, is quite sufficient to lift up our spirits to something of that holy amazement which they must feel, when they see and hear how he pleads for his church. Such will and must be the effect of witnessing his actual intercession, that no witness of it could be unwilling to return to the earth for a time, (were a return proper in all other respects,) just to pay *due honor* to that intercession.

www.ingramcontent.com/pod-product-compliance
Lightning Source LLC
Chambersburg PA
CBHW030322080526
44584CB00012B/662